THE YEAR
OF THE
WHALE

DECORATIONS BY

Leonard Everett Fisher

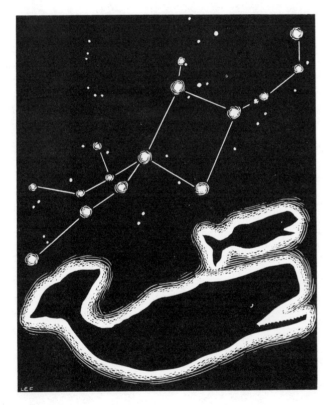

THE YEAR

OF THE

WHALE

By Victor B. Scheffer

New York · CHARLES SCRIBNER'S SONS

Cover illustration: Northern circumpolar constellations—
Ursa Minor, Draco, Ursa Major

A—1.71 [C]

Printed in the United States of America
SBN684-71886-3
Library of Congress Catalog Card Number 68-57084

We need another and a wiser and perhaps a more mystical concept of animals. Remote from universal nature, and living by complicated artifice, man in civilization surveys the creatures through the glass of his knowledge and sees thereby a feather magnified and the whole image in distortion. We patronize them for their incompleteness, for their tragic fate of having taken form so far below ourselves. And therein we err, and greatly err. For the animal shall not be measured by man. In a world older and more complete than ours they move finished and complete, gifted with extensions of the senses we have lost or never attained, living by voices we shall never hear. They are not brethren; they are not underlings; they are other nations, caught with ourselves in the net of life and time, fellow prisoners of the splendour and travail of the earth.

HENRY BESTON—*The Outermost House*

Preface

THIS story of a sperm whale is fiction based on fact. Some of the human characters that appear in it are real, if disguised; others are not real, though they could be. The other whales, the porpoises and dolphins, the fishes and squids, the seabirds, the weather, the kinds of ships, the floating wreckage, the icebergs, the oceanic islands belong to the environment of a sperm whale. When I depart from the story to give information about the study of whales, about whaling, past and present, about conservation, and other related matters, this information is printed in different type from that used for the story. My sources of information appear in the Reference Notes, pages 199–204. These notes include sources of quotations and documentation of factual material and also explain the origins of fictional people and ships. To avoid interrupting the text with reference numbers, the notes are identified by the number of the page and the line or lines to which they refer. In addition, I have provided a special kind of bibliography, confined to some classic works in the literature of whales and whaling.

Each chapter is named for a month of the year, and the decoration by Leonard Everett Fisher that opens each chapter depicts the zodiacal constellation of that month and a different position or activity of the Little Calf or his companions as described in the text. So the sky of September shows Libra; October, Scorpius; November, Sagittarius; December, Capricornus; January, Aquarius; February, Pisces; March, Aries; April, Taurus; May, Gemini; June, Cancer; July, Leo; and August, Virgo. The decoration on the title page shows some winter constellations visible in the Northern Hemisphere—Andromeda and Pegasus. These decorations are not meant as a measurable astronomical chart of the heavens but are purely ornamental, expressing the mystery and wildness of a whale's life.

VICTOR B. SCHEFFER

Contents

THE YEAR
OF THE
WHALE

Prologue:

APPROACHING
THE YEAR
OF THE WHALE

This decade may go down in history as marking the end of life for the largest animal ever to inhabit this earth. If so, it will be another morbid monument to man's short-sighted exploitation of the world's wildlife bounty.

STEWART L. UDALL
Former United States Secretary of the Interior

STEWART UDALL is speaking of the great blue whale. He is saying that we all should be concerned about creatures other than ourselves, though many of them lie beyond our own experience and even beyond our own time. He is saying that we ought to respect the end-twigs of the enormous Tree of Life, ever-growing, now three billion years of age. If we let the blue whale and its kind disappear forever, can we hope for the existence and onward evolution of our own species? If we condone violence toward the whale, leading to the death of the last survivor, will we condone increasing violence in human affairs?

With a sense of urgency I write about another kind of whale, before whales are remembered only from fading photographs and flickering videotapes. I write about the sperm whale, indeed the grandest of the toothed cetaceans.

Why this particular one? Partly because it is quickly identified by the whale hunters and is not confused with other species; the many eyewitness stories of its peculiar habits are unusually reliable.

It is large (up to sixty feet); it has no back fin; it has a huge squarish head almost one-third the length of its body, and a single nostril, which means that it gives off only one spout with each breath. These features are clearly marked.

Its body "can be compared to little else than a dark rock, or the bole of some giant tree," wrote Frederick D. Bennett, an English surgeon who took a whaling voyage in the 1830s.

The sperm whale is cosmopolitan. It roams through all the wild seas of the world except those within the icy borders of the Arctic and Antarctic. Because it is wide-ranging, the chances of finding and studying stranded specimens are correspondingly rich.

The sperm whale has held for mankind a special, mystical meaning from the time of *Moby-Dick* down to today. Moving through a dim, dark, cool, watery world of its own, the whale is timeless and ancient; part of our common heritage and yet remote, awful, prowling the ocean floor a half-mile down, under the guidance of powers and senses we are only beginning to grasp.

"The sperm whale, scientific or poetic, lives not complete in any literature. Far above all other hunted whales, his is an unwritten life," said Herman Melville.

No man can say that he has probed deeply into the natural history of this whale or any whale. And indeed how could he? How could he follow a whale on the high seas through a yearly migration that may—in the example of the gray whale —circle for nine thousand miles, at one extreme among ice floes and at the other under a burning Mexican sun?

The whale biologist does the best he can. He scrapes a film of alga scum from the back of a harpooned animal towed to a whaling station and surmises that the animal had recently lived in colder waters, where this kind of alga is known to flourish. He slices the ovaries of a whale, counts the scars of pregnancy, and reconstructs in imagination the reproductive history and age of the beast. Or he counts the ripple marks on the roots of the teeth, or on the whalebone plates, or on the earwax plug, as a forester counts rings on the butt of a tree, and arrives at another estimate of age. He reads that a sperm whale has tangled in a telephone cable on the sea floor at a depth of over three thousand feet, and he gets new insight into the astounding diving ability of the whale. He finds a mother whale, dead in giving birth, white-blanketed with gulls, at final rest on a sandy beach. The head of the baby protrudes from her body. After a twinge of pity he notes in his record book: "Sperm whale, cephalic presentation."

On such evidence the science of cetology, or whale lore, has been erected. It deals not only with whales but with their smaller relatives the dolphins and porpoises. All are mammals, warm-blooded, giving milk, breathing air. The larger species are known as whales; among the smaller species those with sharp snouts are usually called dolphins, those with blunt heads porpoises. There is a unique species called the narwhal, which has only one tooth, a spiral tusk up to eight feet long, but since this species lives in Arctic waters only, its members do not cross the path of the sperm whales.

In describing the lives of a little sperm whale and his companions I have drawn on the best and newest information. I confess, however, that zoologists are still uncertain about the reproductive cycle, the rate of body growth, and many other aspects of the biology of his species. The four-year cycle of reproduction seems to be most common. A female in the Northern Hemisphere conceives in May of year I, gives birth in September of year II after a gestation period of sixteen months, nurses her calf for two years, or until September of year IV, rests for eight months, and is reimpregnated in May of Year V. Some females, though, are apparently on a two-year cycle and they are reimpregnated in May of year III while they are still nursing. The months mentioned are the peak or popular months for breeding activity, but the breeding time is not sharply defined; the pairing season may in fact extend for eight months and the birth season a corresponding length of time. No one knows whether an individual female

6

can alternate between a two-year and a four-year cycle or can shift to an entirely different cycle. And no one knows the relationship between the age of the female and her current cycle.

The growth rate of the sperm whale will be understood only when we have better methods of estimating age. The light and dark layers of ivory that are visible in the teeth of the whale are surely correlated with age, though whether two or four layers are deposited each year is a moot question. The two-layer plan seems to fit the growth rate of North Pacific sperm whales. It means that both male and female whales reach sexual maturity at about age nine, full body size at perhaps age thirty to forty-five, and extreme old age at seventy-five years.

It is difficult to think about whales without thinking about men; the devoted men who study whales and whaling over the world and who write about them in a dozen languages. I am privileged to know and to communicate with a few of these. The sympathetic thing about them is their pervading interest in conserving whales, not merely their particular skills and interests in zoology. As I write about one particular whale, I try to show, too, how men feel about whales and what they do to whales, and what whales do to men.

As the starting point of the year of the whale I have chosen a quiet month in autumn in the northeastern Pacific Ocean, where a sperm whale calf is born.

SEPTEMBER

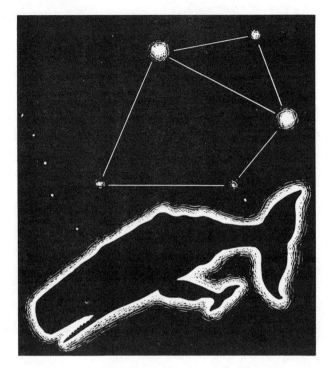

IT is early September when for the first time the Little
Calf sees light—a blue-green, dancing light. He slips easily
from his mother's body beneath the surface of the Pacific
Ocean two hundred miles west of Mexico, on the Tropic of
Cancer. He trembles, for the water is cold and he has lain for
sixteen months in a warm chamber at ninety-six degrees. He
gasps for air as his mother nudges him anxiously to the surface

with her broad snout. He breathes rapidly and desperately for a while, puffing with each breath a small cloud of vapor down the autumn breeze.

The sky above vibrates with a piercing clarity that we who live in the shadow of city smoke have long forgotten. Scattered over the riffled surface of the water as far as the eye can see are small groups of whales. A black back rolls slowly in the sun and glistens for an instant as it disappears. Vapor plumes rise and dissolve in the distance. An occasional *thwack* like a rifle shot breaks the calm, its source a mystery, perhaps a love pat or a mock battle between cavorting youngsters. No bird is in the air, but suddenly, as if by magic, an albatross appears and drops heavily to the water, tearing the surface for twenty yards with its broad webbed feet. It has sighted a fresh, purple-red placenta. Here, on the calving grounds of the sperm whale, the season of birth is at its height.

Whales share with sea cows (manatees and dugongs) and with the hippopotamus of Africa the distinction of being the only mammals born under water. The Little Calf is born tail first, like all young whales, though most human babies, calves, and colts are born head first. Because of his tadpole shape, large head, stiff neck, and long tapering rear, he has no choice but to back into the outer world. There is no time to spare in his birth and no time to correct a mistake. Only for a moment is the baby whale in danger of being trapped in the birth passage or choked by the five-foot umbilical cord.

As mother and calf roll in the wash the cord snaps. The baby opens a pink mouth with knobby, toothless gums and seems suddenly to smile, for the upturned corners of his mouth break into a satisfied smirk. This is illusion, of course; the smile of a whale is a built-in feature with which it is endowed at birth and retains throughout life. A land creature may yawn and snarl and frown, may screw up its forehead and grow wrinkled in old age; the face of the whale stays round and firm—expressionless but for the rolling of the eyes and the clapping of the jaws.

In body form the Little Calf is shapely like his mother, though his tail flukes are pale and crumpled and folded at the corners. While in the womb he had lain like a bent bow, his back arched. Now he is straight and supple. He is almost black, with splotches of white and gray on his slick, rubbery body.

Most whales are in fact dressed in monotonous patterns of black, gray, and white, relieved here and there with faint washes of pink or yellowish. They have no need for brighter coloring, since, as far as anyone knows, they have poor color vision.

In the meantime, off to the north, twenty pilot whales come roistering in with soft explosions, all abreast like troopers. Their foaming wake and the *chuff-chuff-chuff* of their breathing startle the Little Calf. He presses to his mother's side. She makes no move, and the school tumbles on toward the horizon. Had these been killer whales, though, she would have sensed the special underwater sounds of the raiders a mile or more away and would have been ready for battle.

The members of the family of the Little Calf are cruising

in a wide circle which will bring them back in a week to the same spot. Here and there a whale rests at the surface with full stomach, while others move ahead. A triangle tail rises high in the air for a moment as a whale gains momentum for his long descent, or "sound." The placid water roils at the scene of a petty skirmish between two jealous mothers, each with new-born calf. In the still air of the afternoon the little sounds are few and far between, like the whisperings of a desert land, though the sea below is all aquiver with subdued noise—the ultrasounds of a thousand whales communicating with one another and holding their group together by invisible cords. The whales forge slowly ahead, feeding and loafing and play-ing, quarreling a bit but leading in general a quiet life. The time of excitement is six full months away—the season of courtship.

🐬🐬🐬

THE Little Calf on the Tropic of Cancer is far more advanced in body development than any newborn human child. He is wide-eyed, alert, and fully able to swim. Every whale of every kind is in fact precocious at birth; it has to be, for within brief moments it finds itself awash in a grown-up world—no nest, no den, no shelter except the dark shadow of the mother floating beside it. As a zoologist, I use the word "precocious" to mean well-developed in body. This attribute is normal for many birds and mammals, and not an aberration in the hu-man sense.

SEPTEMBER

The greatest advantage to a sea mammal in being large at birth is in keeping warm. The greater the body volume, of course, the slower the heat loss to the chilly sea. The smallest of all cetaceans is the newborn harbor porpoise, with a weight of fifteen pounds. The largest is the adult blue whale, which weighs up to one hundred and seventy-six tons, or as much as two thousand men. We would look in vain in the fossil record of the earth for counterparts of small land mammals for which the names "sea mice" or "sea rabbits" would be appropriate. They could not exist, now or in the past.

An average sperm whale calf at birth is fourteen feet long and weighs a ton; a mother whale is thirty-eight feet long and weighs sixteen tons. How do I know? Opportunities for weighing a newborn whale are exceedingly rare, and the prospect of weighing a full-grown mother is staggering. When any whale is brought to a commercial whaling deck there is little time for biology; business is business; profit is profit; the carcass must be turned into meal and oil and frozen meat without delay. If the whale is a pregnant female, the government biologist, present with his measuring tape and specimen jars, is itching to have his hands on the fetus for just an hour. If the whaling foreman says okay, he can; if not, the unborn baby will go into the cooking pot along with the mother, or over the rail into the sea with the entrails.

Occasionally, a biologist has a chance to study a fetus or a newborn whale. Though newborn whales cannot legally be killed, from time to time they are cast up by the sea in fresh condition or even alive, stranded where they can be seen. Then the biologist is happy as he probes and peers, takes photographs and measurements, plops things into alcohol. Finally he builds a tripod of driftwood and hoists the whale, chunk by chunk, upon his weighing scale. As evening falls he heads for home, tired and bloody, with a small skull tied to the fender of his car, to be greeted by a tolerant wife and a sniffing dog.

About the time that our Little Calf was born, another sperm whale baby, alone and in deep trouble, was swimming through a weedy channel in another sea. Four natives of a Bermuda island chased it in a boat. A man in the bow tried to spear it, then, frustrated, jumped over the side, clothes and all, a manila line in his hand. With long experience as a fisherman he looped the line deftly around the baby's tail. The sweating men towed the protesting creature to a small cove where they exhibited it alive for two days—admission one half crown.

A visitor from the Oceanographic Station watched the whale as it died of overheating. An English biologist with experience at sea, he concluded, from the size of the animal and the fresh pink of the umbilical scar, that he was looking at what few men have seen, a sperm whale near time of birth. The native owners, for a slight fee, postponed the butchering until the scientist could return with his watercolors, sketchpad, and measuring tape.

The baby proved to be thirteen feet three inches long from snout to base of tail notch. Its color pattern was soon recorded, and a year later its smiling face appeared in a scientific journal—the only picture of its kind.

〰〰〰

ON his first day of life the Little Calf blunders round and round his mother's body, seeking blindly for the place he finally finds: a soft spot that tastes good when he nuzzles it. Each of the mother's two nipples is hidden in a deep slit, one on each side of the belly, far behind the navel. He works his little mouth into position and presses hard; his mother responds by extruding one nipple at a time and squirting a strong flow of milk against the back of his throat. Occasionally the mother turns on her side, with her breast nearly out of the water while the calf, lying parallel with his head in the same direction, holds the teat sideways in the angle of his jaw with his snout protruding from the surface. Such an arrangement seems very awkward, for the Little Calf has no real lips and his lower jaw is narrow, underslung, and twenty inches long.

In his first struggle to nurse, the Little Calf is hindered by a grown female playing the role of "auntie." She lost her own calf by miscarriage in July. With the keen sense of group solidarity of sperm whales, she senses that something is wrong. She glides up to the pair and time and again places her long body between mother and calf. Each time, she is repulsed with a blow from the mother's flukes. She finally moves to a safe distance and listens to the submarine click-talk between the pair, the tones of the mother strong and steady, those of the baby weak and experimental.

For two years the Little Calf will continue to suck at his mother's belly, rising and dipping near the surface of the sea in the long Pacific swell. He follows his mother like a shadow and grows rapidly on his diet of thick milk, over one-third of it pure fat. (The blue dairy milk delivered to my doorstep each morning contains only four percent fat.) His coat of blubber is only an inch thick at first, and during the first few weeks he shivers in the chill of the sea. He will grow steadily throughout the long suckling period, gaining an average of seven pounds a day. Many years hence his blubber coat will have developed into a great firm blanket more than a foot thick.

By the end of September the Little Calf is able to match the speed of his family. When a Panama freighter comes throbbing near, alarming the group, he leaps actively beside his mother, spouting freely, keeping up well with the rapid pace of the retreating party. One of the half-grown males bursts clear of the water and floats for an instant against the dark blue sky before he twists in midair and crashes on his side in a glorious fountain of white. Another catches the spirit and breaches four times in a row; he finally coasts along near the surface, tired but content.

But the Little Calf does not fare so well one morning in late September when the sky turns black and sullen, the wind rises, and the fringes of the waves begin to tear away in ragged sheets. The chatter of his family is lost to him in the scream of the gale. One moment beside his mother, at the next he is lifted in a smother of foam, then down a dark, dizzy, sliding trough deep into the sea before he can gasp for breath or clear his nose. His mother senses the trouble and makes a lee for him with her great, comforting back. He spouts air and water for several minutes, then breathes more freely, falls in with the smashing rhythm of the seas, and feels secure. All that day and night his mother stays with him.

Ordinarily, she would have made a dozen or more deep

dives during the night to feast on fish and squid. This she must do to replenish her milk supply. It is no hardship, though, for her to fast for a night, for like all whales she can go for weeks without food, living on the reserve fat in her body. Not content perhaps, she is accepting, suffused with what we humans call mother love. Like many a denizen of the open sea she has ridden out a hundred storms, wherein to feed or try to feed would be more painful than simply to wait.

The sky clears in the new dawn. The members of the family convene and begin to doze or play under the warm rays of the sun. A great sea, two hundred feet from crest to crest, is running as slick and silent as oil.

A whale "family" is a loose social group of about thirty whales. It is never the same from one month to the next. It is part of a great school consisting of many families. The family of the Little Calf includes young males and young females, pregnant cows, nursing cows with calves, and an old bull who is usually a half-mile to windward from the nursery. The social pattern of this group has long been familiar to whale hunters, who call it a "harem." At the breeding place the adult females outnumber the adult males, and the males are distinctly larger than the females. Both features are typical of polygamous animals. One might think that sperm whales have been forced into this social scheme in order to gain mutual protection in the harsh and boundless sea, except for the fact that some kinds of whales seem to live solitary lives, with no apparent social structure.

One day follows another as the nights grow longer and the morning sea fogs of late summer are swept away by the clear winds of autumn. Through September, in waters from Mexico to the Hawaiian Islands, swollen cows are bringing forth their young; some even in October. Far to the north in the Bering Sea and along the Aleutian Islands, the bachelor males and solitary bulls are feeding. Fat and warm-coated, they are in no hurry to turn southward for the winter. Virgin females have been feeding off British Columbia. They now feel the chill of fall in the currents of the North Pacific Drift and turn slowly toward the tropics. Scattered among them are mothers attended by suckling calves, one year or two years old.

The migrations of the whales, their movements from season to season, their integration with the family at one time and separation at another, their sense of belonging with companions of similar age, sex, and breeding experience, all suggest that a multitude of signals from the world around are constantly reaching their minds through ears, eyes, skin, and doubtless other perceptual channels as yet undiscovered. The life of a whale is surely complex, and by no means as monotonous as one might think. The daily task of living involves far more than rising to breathe, sinking to feed, staring at a liquid plain, and swimming . . . swimming . . . swimming.

In the group of cows straggling southward from Vancouver Island is one who keeps rudely shoving her calf aside, indicating that she has lost all interest in the role of nursing mother. Her calf is now two years old—a great, hulking, twenty-four-footer with a weight of nearly four tons. Of late he has adopted the annoying habit of tearing food from her mouth as she rises from the deep with struggling fishes in her grasp. Earlier she felt the instinctive rightness of sharing her food with her calf; now she feels that it is time for him to shove off for good. Furthermore, she happens to be one of the cows who is on a two-year rather than a four-year breeding cycle; she was bred again when her calf was only four months old. For the past sixteen months she has been nourishing a small life within her body and another one without. No wonder she is weary of motherhood!

As the Little Calf grows daily more aware of his world he is fascinated by the actions of the harem bull (his father, unbeknownst), the great, black, sixty-ton beast who guards the perimeter of the family circle. The bull is often absent for an hour or more on some mysterious errand. Where does he go so quickly in broad daylight on an open sea? Down, down, on a long, slanting course through the zones of green and purple twilight to utter blackness below. Luminescent fishes and strange blobby creatures brush past his undulating tail as he goes steadily deeper. The pressure is now one hundred tons to the square foot; the water is deathly cold and quiet. At a depth of three thousand feet he levels off and begins to search for prey. The sonar device in his great dome is operating at full peak. Within a quarter-hour he reads an attractive series of echoes and he turns quickly to the left, then to the right. Suddenly he smashes into a vague, rubbery, pulsating wall. The acoustic signal indicates the center of the Thing. He swings open his gatelike lower jaw with its sixty teeth, seizes the prey, clamps it securely in his mouth, and shoots for the surface. He has found a half-grown giant squid, thirty feet long, three hundred pounds in weight. The squid writhes in torment and tries to tear at its captor, but its sucking tentacles slide from the smooth, rushing body. When its parrot beak touches the head of the whale it snaps shut and cuts a small clean chunk of black skin and white fibrous tissue. The whale shakes its prey in irritation.

Suddenly the surrounding water fills with light and the bull lies puffing in the sunshine. He crushes the squid's central spark of life, its gray tentacles twist and roll obscenely like dismembered snakes. The Little Calf watches in excitement as the bull begins to breathe in great gasping drafts, expelling each breath in a pyramid of vapor which holds not only stale air and moisture but also a special kind of foam or mucus. Patches of this dry like meringue on the top of his head before he is done with breathing—fifty breaths or more. Now at ease, the bull turns to the dead beast and leisurely chomps it into bite-size pieces, each the size of a football, and thrusts them mechanically into his gullet with muscular tongue.

𝕊𝕊𝕊

ABOVE my desk there hangs a pen-and-ink reproduction of "The Kraken Supposed a Sepia Or Cuttle Fish." A sailing ship of the 1600s is heeled over on her beam by the weight of a sea monster, a gray thing resembling mushroom, toad, snake, and giant squash. Tentacles the size of forest trees are twined around the mast and sails and flag. Brave men slash with broadaxes at the slithering arms; others less brave but wiser leap from the deck into the sea. Gulls settle from the sky, anticipating a feast on human bits. What is the "kraken"?

The kraken is a Norwegian mythological monster which dwells in caverns measureless to man. When all the evidence is sorted I am sure that it is a giant squid, and I believe that it must be the largest animal without a backbone on earth, up to sixty feet long and weighing more than a ton. The largest ones stare into the watery dimness with cold eyes fifteen inches in diameter.

The Norwegians tell an old story about a bishop of Nidaros who conducted a seaside service on the back of a sleeping kraken, mistaking it for a rock. He set up his altar and gave such an eloquent sermon that when the monster awoke it remained quiet until the good man had folded his altar and left.

Were I not a scientist I should like to believe with Tennyson that:

Below the thunders of the upper deep,
Far, far beneath in the abysmal sea,
His ancient, dreamless, uninvaded sleep
The Kraken sleepeth; faintest sunlights flee
About his shadowy sides; above him swell
Huge sponges of millennial growth and height;
And far away into the sickly light,
From many a wondrous grot and secret cell
Unnumber'd and enormous polypi
Winnow with giant arms the slumbering green.

There hath he lain for ages, and will lie
Battening upon huge sea-worms in his sleep,
Until the latter fire shall heat the deep;
Then once by man and angels to be seen,
In roaring he shall rise and on the surface die.

OCTOBER

O N a morning in early October the sea is glass, without a ripple or sound. A feather falls from the breast of an albatross winging its lonely way northwestward to the Leeward Islands and home. The plume drifts lightly to the sea and comes to rest on a mirror image. It is a day when time itself is still.

At the first glow of dawn the Little Calf and a companion of his own age have filled their bellies with warm milk. Now they are looking for fun. A vague tingling, an unquiet, grows in the water about them. For a while they pass it off as porpoise talk, a part of the daily world, a murmur as common as the lapping of waves. But ever more clearly a pulsating beat comes through the sea. In unison the whales flex their muscular bodies and surge ahead to gain velocity. In a rush they raise their stubby heads above the water and gaze quickly but intently toward the horizon, right and left. (They cannot look straight ahead, for their eyes are on their sides.) A half-mile away they dimly see the flashing bodies of white-sided dolphins at play, bursting the placid sea and scattering a million jewels behind. The dolphins are hot in pursuit of a low-hulled gray ship, a ship flying the Navy jack and moving on a zigzag course at six knots.

The little whales drop heavily into the water and take off at full speed toward the fun. (In later years they will learn to fear the sound of men and ships; now they are young and reckless.)

The ship is the *Shark*, a training ship for antisubmarine warfare, carrying recruits who are learning both to echolocate, or range, and to listen for the sounds of enemy craft ranging in turn for *them*. Below deck a chief and fifteen men are sitting in a darkened room, their faces dimly lit by the green glow of an oscilloscope. A loudspeaker in the ceiling is crackling in a torrent of nonhuman sound. Squeaks, squawks, whistles, hums, and clipping notes are interlaced with the steady "ping-ping-ping" of the ship's transmitter.

OCTOBER

"Those are dolphins coming in," says the chief, "and I'll put them on tape for a playback after lunch. I'll run them along with the fish records we picked up outside San Diego." He describes each characteristic sound and its word-picture on the glowing screen. The sounds are not voices; they are vibrations. They are not made by vocal cords and are largely inaudible to the human ear without the aid of instruments—that is to say, they range in shrillness to nearly ten times the upper hearing limit of a sharp-eared human being.

As the small whales close in, the dolphins are at the bow. They are having a wonderful time, though the ship is not zipping along as fast as they would wish. One dolphin takes delight in crowding his companions, one by one, to the clean prow cutting the water, forcing them to flip explosively or else be run down.

The racket of the loudspeaker is unbearable and the chief turns down the volume. From the bridge comes a message that twenty or so dolphins are playing around the ship. (It is hard to count them, for some are running submerged.) "I've got a man at the peak taking movies," says the skipper. When the vessel returns to port, the film will be developed, the species will be identified by the whale expert at the University, and the sound track will be properly labeled as to source. It will eventually be duplicated and sent to sound libraries in Navy installations all over the country.

As the volume dies the chief frowns and holds up his hand for silence. He fiddles with the knobs. Another "ping-

ping-ping"—erratic, now loud, now faint, like the distant noise of carpenters shingling a roof or men beating a boiler with hammers—comes in. He shuts off the ship's own pinger and asks a recruit to phone the bridge. Is another ship coming in?

In a moment he has the answer: two small whales are running alongside about a hundred yards off the starboard beam. "They're sperm," the skipper adds, for he has turned with an inquiring glance to the bos'n, an old-timer who once served a hitch on a whale-catcher out of Eureka, California.

"Listen sharp," says the chief to his men. "I've never heard a sperm before, at least for sure, but during the war I had a couple of bad times on a PYC, wondering whether to call for a depth charge. Both times, the sound wasn't quite right for a sub and I sweated it out."

Now coffee circulates in heavy mugs and the wardroom talk turns to the underwater sounds of cetaceans, how the slapping of tail flukes or flippers may resemble a ship's propeller, and how the resonant phonations may simulate the noise of instruments.

"The body origin of whale sound is poorly known," continues the chief. "Sometimes a man in the open air can hear a whale talking and can even see bubbles rising from its mouth or nose. I personally don't think the bubbles have any connection with the source of sound. From what I have read, the sound is like the screech you hear when you partway turn on a kitchen faucet with a leaky gasket. The source is 'cavitation,' or a string of vacuum bubbles in liquid."

OCTOBER

A sharp recruit suggests that it might be possible to disguise a submarine as a whale by playing back, underwater, the proper pulse trains. The chief smiles. "Maybe you've got something there. I'll give you another idea about as practical: the ideal hiding place for a sub would be at a depth of two hundred feet, among echoing shoals and rocks, just below a thermocline—a sharp change in water density—and underneath a school of whales. That setup would be guaranteed to fool the smartest man at the listening post."

The chief turns on the *Shark*'s pinger again and the hammering duet of the Little Calf and his companion fades away. The whales, irritated by the unfamiliar staccato ping of the monster they are shadowing, have lost interest. They start back to seek the quiet of the family, which now seems to be a frightful distance away. The small whales have learned a lesson in time and space.

ʃʃʃ

UNDERWATER communication and range-finding by whales is a new field, called "ketophonation," which means "whale-produced vibrations."

One often hears that animals communicate with each other, and of course they do, but not in the sense that humans talk or signal or gesture in certain deliberate ways for the purpose of getting certain responses. When I see a stray dog sniffing the shrubbery at my doorstep I shout "Beat it!" and wave my arms. I predict with reliability what the result will be. When my own dog Tucker sees the stray he barks furiously and leaps after him. The end result is the same in each case: the invader reads the signal and retreats.

The important difference is that I know what will happen but Tucker *does not*. If the invader were ten times his size, Tucker would give chase with the same abandon, while I would think twice before responding. When Tucker sees a specific situation his instinctive trigger is pulled and the chase is on, willy-nilly.

Most of what is known about echo-location, or sonar ranging by whales came to light in the early years of the Second World War, the desperate years when scientists of maritime nations were listening to the submarine sounds of enemy ships, as well as to strange, and at that time unidentified, sounds of fishes, crabs, shrimps, seals, porpoises, and whales. There is now a bibliography of more than a thousand scientific reports on underwater noises of biological origin.

In 1947, Arthur F. McBride of Marineland, near St. Augustine, Florida, observed that porpoises were able to sense the difference between a fine-mesh net and a coarse-mesh net in murky waters at night. He suspected that this behavior must be associated with some highly specialized mechanism enabling the porpoise to learn a great deal about its environment through sound.

In 1949, William E. Schevill and Barbara Lawrence of Harvard University first recorded on tape the underwater sounds of an identified cetacean. They had deliberately set out to stalk the beluga or white whale, for among seafaring men it has long been known as the "sea canary." Its trilling voice, produced under water, can be heard in the open air. The researchers were indeed able to capture this trill, as well as the variety of whistles, squeaks, ticks, and clucks. They reported that occasionally the calls suggested a crowd of children shouting in the distance.

In the years 1950 to 1958, many aspects of sound production by whales were examined in an atmosphere of rising excitement. Anatomists, psychologists, physicists, and students of animal behavior all contributed to the growing body of knowledge. The cetacean ear was found to be sensitive to frequencies as high as two hundred kilohertz, as compared to the human ear with an upper limit of about twenty. It became clear that the phonations were suitable for echo-location.

Schevill and Lawrence and a trainer worked with a solitary porpoise in a turbid pond, noting the ease with which it came to the trainer for food. They were convinced in 1956 that the beast was using sonar because *no other clue* (sight or sound not made by the porpoise himself) was available.

In 1958 W. N. Kellogg, professor of experimental psychology at Florida State University, described results which left no doubt that captive porpoises in his laboratory were using sonar to discriminate underwater objects. In a final series of one hundred and forty trials, a porpoise named Albert made no errors at all in selecting six-inch fish in preference to twelve-inchers. He made his selections at high speed, as quickly in darkness as in light, and in spite of attempts by Kellogg to jam his sonar with artificial playback of his earlier phonations.

It is useless to argue about who was first to discover sonar in whales; there was no first. Today no one travels alone in the search for truth.

🐟🐟🐟

THE Little Calf is slowly beginning to recognize and to remember certain members of his group. There is a great-aunt whose lower jaw was horribly twisted and nearly broken off years ago in a fight with a killer whale. The tip of her jaw is bent at an angle of forty-five degrees; it juts outside her mouth, all covered with algae and barnacles. She is not bothered by the deformity but continues to swim actively and to catch fish and squids.

Another old cow has seen forty-three winters. She has escaped the whale hunters because she is often with calf, and the hunters will not shoot a nursing mother. Her back is heavily scarred with pale circles ranging in size from that of a teacup to that of a dinner plate. Some of them are made by the powerful sucking disks that fringe the tentacles and arms of the squid and octopus. Other circular marks are reminders of stinging attacks by lampreys, those wriggling, yard-long, slimy brown creatures that repel even the zoologist. The lamprey way of life is to fasten itself to the body of a whale or a fish by means of round, rubbery, sucking lips. The mouth is lined with rasping teeth which leave permanent marks or, from a small and helpless victim, drain the life blood entirely. On whales, the scars are pure circles, hundreds upon hundreds, strewn thickly at random like overlapping craters of the moon.

(A fisheries officer once wrote me from South Africa,

OCTOBER

"Who would have put the numerals 39 in white paint on a porpoise?" What he saw was almost certainly a set of curlicue marks made by the teeth of some marine predator.)

A third female in the Little Calf's group was the victim of a weird accident. On her back, above and behind the right flipper, is a long callused ridge. It will stay there until she dies. If she is killed by a whaling crew, the flensing knife of the butcher will dull itself on a hard thing buried in the ridge. The thing is the bony bill of a swordfish, or broadbill. Four years earlier, on a moonless night, she was cruising off the Bonin Islands when she neared a group of swordfish on a collision course. One of them, a big eight-hundred pounder, took evasive action at the same instant she turned. At a speed of thirty knots the long sword slipped cleanly and smoothly into her back, buried itself in the blubber, and snapped off at the base. The entry wound closed in a few weeks and the sword was entombed.

Another member of the group was attacked deliberately, I think. The evidence for intentional attacks by swordfish goes back to the Second World War when ships carrying bales of rubber were torpedoed in the Mozambique Channel. Many bales drifted ashore. Beachcombers saw that some bales contained the buried tips of spears of marlin and swordfish, as many as four tips to a bale. In one bale there was held firmly a spear tip two feet long, representing a four-hundred-pound marlin, along with the embedded teeth of a great white shark. Poor marlin! He had struggled in vain to withdraw his beak; he was attacked by sharks; and one of the sharks in a frenzy of blood lust had sunk his razor teeth into the bale. The bale carried ashore the mementos of the struggle.

In 1967 a swordfish punctured the hull of a submarine. The mini-sub *Alvin*, cruising off Georgia at a depth of eighteen hundred feet, was rammed so hard that the swordfish could not withdraw its thirty-inch bill. The crew brought the craft to the surface, pried the bill out of the hull, and fried the choicer parts of the fish for dinner.

(Of the swordfish, Oppian of Cilicia in A.D. 180 remarked, as translated, "Nature her bounty to his mouth confined, gave him a sword, but left unarmed his mind.")

Other members of the whale group are less plainly marked, but the Little Calf can identify them also. Each has a scar pattern, skin pigment, and click-voice. All the older whales have been repeatedly scratched and bitten around the face by beaks of giant squids. These horny mouthparts, which can sever a man's finger, leave long white marks on the thin black epidermis of the whales. Covering the background of the skin is often a maze of white lines, straight and curved—graffiti, the tangled tracks of a thousand attacks by rasping beaks and horny teeth and scratching, clawing feet.

One of the older females has a dent on her forehead from a collision with the sea floor. Traveling at high speed in pursuit of an angler fish, in inky darkness a half-mile down, she grazed a rocky pinnacle.

Another younger female has a skin furrow where a harpoon fired by an apprentice whaler struck the water at a low angle and skipped along her back without exploding.

Still another carries in her backside a rare souvenir: a stainless-steel tube with Russian lettering, a tracer mark implanted by a biologist of the research vessel *Aleut*, out of the Vladivostok Marine Station.

Now a strange female joins the group, a whale newly arrived from the warmer waters of the south. The Little Calf circles her warily. Sprouting from her back and sides are a dozen creatures, sickly gray in color, sixteen inches long—fish, to be sure, but not quite proper fish. One of them falls softly from the body of the whale and swims with feeble strokes toward the Little Calf. On the top of the creature's head there is a long oval pattern of fleshy treads like the sole of a yachting shoe. It is a suction pad—adhesive disk—and the creature is a whale sucker or remora. In the long course of evolution this kind of organism has given up its freedom and part of its muscular strength in exchange for the comfort of hitchhiking on larger animals. Attachment has become a way of life. Without a host upon which to fasten, the remora is doomed, for in the open sea it cannot long escape the rush of its enemies: sharks and barracudas.

The Little Calf darts away and the gray creature sinks, flopping down and deeper down. On the following day, the visitor from the south is nearly rid of her fellow travelers. A week later all are gone; her skin is clean. The water is too cold for their comfort and they have cut loose, to die or to fasten to a southbound host.

On a chill, drizzly day in mid-October the Little Calf sees emerging from the mist a strange craft. This is the *Orchid*, designed by scientists for sea research and photography. She is cruising at her usual speed of seven knots. Suddenly the telegraph signals FULL ASTERN. The vessel shudders; the dishes fly in the galley; the chairs in the saloon bring up with a crash against the fore wall.

Thrashing in the wake of the screw is a smallish, ten-ton female whale. She was dozing peacefully at the surface, barely awash, dead ahead, while the man at the wheel of the *Orchid* stared at a spout off the starboard bow. She is the young female who carries in her backside the stainless-steel marker with the strange device. It will never get back to Vladivostok, for the bearer is mortally injured. She sends out a wild, ragged call of distress and two of her companions move in. They defecate in sympathy. They put their shoulders under her body on either side and try to support her at the surface. Other whales come from all sides, showing the instinctive care-giving behavior of cetaceans that biologists once scoffed at but now accept as real.

꣼꣼꣼

LONG before biologists began to write complicated sentences about care-giving behavior, commercial whalers knew how to exploit it for profit. They would wound a whale calf, knowing that the mother would come to its rescue, at which time both mother and calf could be killed. A watercolor painted in 1840, now in the Whaling Museum at New Bedford, Massachusetts, shows a mother sperm whale rearing from the sea with her dying calf held crosswise in her jaws, a harpoon trailing from the bloody flank of the little one.

When the famous Marine Studios at Marineland, Florida, built the first large aquarium to show porpoises under water, biologists moved quickly to the scene with notebooks and cameras. One of their first rewards was an insight into care-giving. A young porpoise had died during the night, and the next morning they saw its mother patiently supporting the lifeless body at the surface as though helping it to breathe.

In the light of this and other observations it is hard for me to be coldly scientific. I glow at the thought that here may be displayed the kind of behavior which, a million years ago in the Olduvai Gorge, turned the direction of a subhuman beast toward the narrow avenue which has led to social man.

At about the time of the Marine Studios event, a true-life story by a Florida woman was published in a popular science magazine.

"My adventure with a porpoise occurred six years ago. . . .

"We had at the time a narrow beach, reached by a flight of slippery and a bit rickety steps. When I went out to my cabana, no one was in sight, nor did anyone appear when I went swimming. . . .

"The waves were not over two feet high, and I waded out just waist deep before I realized that there was a terrific undertow. Just as I started to turn back, the undertow swept my feet from under me and knocked me flat in the water. I swallowed a lot of water and, in spite of repeated tries, could not get my footing. I tried to call, but between the water in my lungs and my real fright, I suppose my voice was not loud enough. I realized that, while only about ten feet from shore, there was no way I could make it, and I kept thinking, as I gradually lost consciousness, please God can't someone push me ashore.

"With that, someone gave me a tremendous shove, and I landed on the beach, face down, too exhausted to turn over. I kept thinking that I must turn over and thank the person who helped me. It was several minutes before I could do so, and when I did, no one was near, but in the water about eighteen feet out a porpoise was leaping around, and a few feet beyond him another large fish was also leaping.

"When I got enough energy to get back up the steps, a man who had been standing on the other side of the fence on the public beach came running over. He asked me how I was and said that he had seen only the last part. It was the second time, he asserted, that he had seen such a thing happen. He said that when he had arrived, I looked like a dead body and that the porpoise shoved me ashore. It was his belief that the porpoise was trying to protect me from the other fish, which he described as a fishtail shark. God certainly was with me."

❧❧❧

IN the haunts of the Little Calf, a crew of adventurers on the brigantine *Fairy* are homeward bound from Easter Island to California. The ship moves slowly under sail, her motor stilled. The crew doze, or mend clothes, or polish tackle.

Suddenly a cry breaks from the wheelhouse, half in jest, "Tha-a-a-r she blo-o-o-ws and sparm at that!" There is a swift patter of bare feet on deck, a rush to the bow. The *Fairy* has penetrated to the very center of the Little Calf's group. Whales churn out in all directions, one passing so close to the *Fairy* that the rank smell of its breath drifts to the nostrils of the men on board. Tremaine, the teen-age son of the captain, is hanging over the bowsprit. He cannot contain his excitement. He grabs a shark iron, a keen-edged harpoon with line and float attached, and seconds later hurls it deep into the back of a small female that slides beneath him. Good God!

The whale is no less astounded than the boy. The line speeds from the bucket like a living thing. "Lower away," cries the captain, and the crew drop a motor launch over the side, with the captain at the wheel and Tremaine at his side. As they near the wounded animal, they hesitate. Three large whales have returned to the scene of action and are circling the victim —she is a yearling half-sister of the Little Calf.

The line parts, though whether from a bite or from the sheer impact of a passing body is not at the moment clear. Tremaine quickly fastens a new line to the bight of the old one and the captain succeeds in planting a second iron near the whale's left flank. Bleeding from both wounds, she moves away in a streak of foam, towing the launch behind her.

Meanwhile, the *Fairy* moves in under full power and two sailors carry rifles up to the peak. They blaze away at the running whale for an hour and are about to quit from exhaustion when they see the line go slack. The lifeless body rolls in a pink wash.

They haul her partly out of the sea with the ship's tackle and a line looped round her flukes. When the winch begins to shudder and whine, they stop—she is far too heavy to handle. They take movies; they strip a long, dark-red, ten-pound sirloin steak from her back and cut her loose to the sharks.

On the eastern edge of the feeding grounds of the Little Calf's family, brown seaweeds, torn from their moorings on the continental shelf in a brutal gale of wind and swept to sea, float in a vast circle. Oozy golden stems hang deep and trailing. They sway in concert, slowly turn and twist; the filtered sunlight threads the tangle and loses itself in the greeny gloom below. Here and there a stem holds in its grasp a round stone, and as the plant dies the stone falls unseen to the floor of the sea, far from its native bed. Streaming on the surface, and all in one direction, bright leaves flow in the current. The ocean is pricked with a million glancing lights where fronds catch the breeze and fold back and forth, back and forth. Brown domes, bulbous floats, nod and jerk like puppet heads. Shore fishes, carried along in the vast confusion of the storm, dart through the sapless foliage, exploring, seizing the tiny creatures that rain from the stems.

Into the floating forest come the Little Calf and his family. Though he has often seen kelp he has never seen such a tremendous bed far at sea in the blue-water zone. He probes the tangle, rolls a mouthful of strands, and spits them out.

OCTOBER

They have a faintly foodlike flavor, but not to his taste. With his little back just below the surface he pushes experimentally into the mass. The stems slither against his skin—not a bad sensation, really. His eyes are useless in the jungle of rippling brown and shade, and his ears pick up a babble of soft echoes. With eyes closed he moves slowly ahead in this new and delightful world. He is driven by a primordial urge to discover, to change pace, to test the environment for possibilities—the urge that powers the motion of evolution. (The motion is often toward a dead end, to be sure.)

When he surfaces after ten minutes he finds that a half-brother has been cruising on a parallel course. Together they rush through the kelp, leaping and twisting, churning the sea into brown foam, trailing streamers behind them, splashing in pure abandon. The fun ends abruptly when the Little Calf rams the broad side of the harem bull and takes a blow from the bull's tail that sends him reeling back to the comfort of his mother. He sneezes loudly, with a flowering of mist.

〰〰〰

IN Washington, D.C., in 1963, fifty men and women came to an international convention for the study of cetaceans. The delegates spoke many languages and had many interests. Some were "pure" scientists fired by the clean white flame of curiosity; others "applied" scientists eager to know more about whales in order to conserve them wisely for the good of mankind. All were trained in the handling of evidence and all were habitual skeptics. Whether they were listening to a whaling anecdote or to the technical report of a controlled experiment, they would ask: "Is the speaker's interpretation true? Can there be a better explanation?"

One session was concerned with the intelligence of cetaceans. Keller Breland, president of Animal Behavior Enterprises, Hot Springs, Arkansas, started it with a definition: "intelligence is the breakdown of the instinctive fixity, increasing the potential for recombination, both within the musculature and in the environment." The listeners agreed that intelligence is the ability to climb out of that evolutionary groove which traps the lower animals and makes them react like machines. However, when the discussion turned to specific tests and rating schemes for intelligence, a lively, good-natured debate ensued.

Arthur F. McBride, mentioned earlier, is highly respected as the pioneer of "oceanariums" in the 1930s. D.O. Hebb, his partner, is a specialist in primate biology and knows a good deal about ways of testing intelligence, especially about the rating of chimpanzees faced with new and strange situations. A summary of their report on the behavior of porpoises follows.

There is no direct evidence concerning the porpoise's intelligence—the average level of his problem solving—and no immediate prospects of obtaining any. In respect to his emotional and motivational behavior, however, the porpoise appears to fall somewhere in the range of development between dog and chimpanzee.

First, porpoises show fear of strange sounds and strange motionless objects. Rats do not. When a bright-colored beach ball is left floating in a porpoise tank, the animals fall silent for a whole day; they stop playing and leaping out of the water.

Second, porpoises seem to make friends with each other, like dogs and chimpanzees, but not like rats.

Third, porpoises play and often amuse themselves for an hour or more with a floating feather, or by teasing a shark, turtle, or pelican in the same tank, or by rhythmically diving and slapping the water. (Does this last, I wonder, resemble the rhythmic dance of the chimpanzee?)

Fourth, porpoises have peculiar sexual habits unrelated to straightforward mating activities. These habits lead to the suspicion that porpoises are "higher" animals, approaching man.

The next speaker, Professor A. Brazier Howell of Johns Hopkins University, stated that "although the porpoise apparently has less need for intelligence than almost any other living mammal . . . the convolutions of its brain are more marked than in man, thus indicating the probability that this character is not as significant of intelligence as many now believe."

According to Tokuzo Kojima, biologist with the Japanese Whales Research Institute, the brain of a fifty-foot sperm whale weighs seventeen pounds. Since a whale of this size weighs forty-two tons, the whole body weight is *five thousand times* that of the brain. By comparison, the brain of an adult man weighs three pounds, and thus the weight of a man is only *fifty or sixty times* that of his brain.

A new look at the brain of the porpoise was provided by zoologists Sam H. Ridgway, N. J. Flanigan, and James G. McCormick, who claimed that the truly critical feature is not the gross weight but the relationship between weight of brain and weight of spinal cord. Roughly speaking, the brain is the center of reasoned behavior; the cord of reflexive. Some of the huge dinosaurs had a brain the size of a walnut, but a massive cord. The team had dissected fifteen porpoises of three species. Their figures on comparative brain-to-cord ratios were: fishes, less than 1; horse, 2.5; cat, 4 or 5; apes, 8; PORPOISES, 36; man, 50. These findings show the porpoise in a favorable light indeed.

The final speaker was John Cunningham Lilly of the Communications Research Institute, Miami, Florida, who stated that, in the first place, no deep-sea cetacean has a brain weighing less than two pounds. Nature has required of cetaceans a certain threshold-number of brain cells (a certain number of computer units), otherwise the animals would not be able to cope with life in the sea. The largest known brain on this planet was one taken from a sperm whale; it weighed over nineteen pounds.

Furthermore, experiments which he had carried out with porpoises suggest that they talk in "dolphinese." He described vocal exchanges between pairs of dolphins which bear a formal resemblance to human conversation in that each animal transmits only during the silences of the other animal. (I would except human females.) If porpoises are held in captivity with humans long enough, these animals gradually modify the noises they emit and gradually acquire new noises which begin to resemble the noises of human speech. (But so do parrots and mynahs.) Lilly asserted that he has no patience with "spiritualists" and "psychics" who maintain that a mind can exist without a body, but he does respect the *unknown mind* in a *known brain*, like the dolphin's.

At the beginning of the conference, Dr. L. Harrison Matthews, director of the Zoological Society of London, made a very pertinent comment: "Now it seems that some people are proposing to prostitute their biological work on the Cetacea and involve the animals in human international strife by training them as underwater watchdogs to guard naval installations from frogmen, or to act as unmanned submarines. Intelligent as the animals may be, they are, unfortunately, not sufficiently intelligent to refuse cooperation and treat their trainers to some of those characteristic underwater noises which, if produced in the air, would be regarded as gestures of contempt."

Cheers, Dr. Matthews!

GLIDING eastward through the entrance to the Strait of Juan de Fuca which leads to Puget Sound, a great-uncle of the Little Calf is following a long procession of chum salmon. The fish are moving steadily to the tributaries of the Fraser River, where they will soon leave their shining eggs in the gravel and die. They are the last of the fall run. It has slowly penetrated the mind of the whale that the fish are increasing by the moment. They are funneling into the sweet ribbons of fresh water that intertwine the salt, each fish in its own mysterious way seeking out the bed that gave it life three or four years ago. All this is beyond the ken of the whale. He knows only that where he once picked up an occasional salmon in an hour of chase he is now in a thick flashing of silver shapes—more fish than he can swallow. Sheer chance has led him east. He passes by the trailing lines of fishermen from Neah Bay and Sekiu and Pysht. He is alone. The others of his group are feeding far at sea, in the blue water beyond sight of Cape Flattery. Warned by ancient instinct, they shun the narrow channel of the Strait.

And well they may, for the quiet pleasure sea of Puget Sound is the year-round home of a pack of killer whales, the largest and swiftest of all the predatory mammals of the sea. At the moment, a group of seventeen searches for prey, led by a nine-ton bull. His splendid pattern is pure black and white; full dress, white tie and tails. As he cuts the surface a bold dorsal fin stands five feet high, like a mast. He and his pack are well known to the yachtsmen who see them cruising and thrill at the sight. The whales take a routine course that carries them north, outside Vancouver Island, then down through Davis Strait and the San Juans. Their food is herring, halibut, hake, and squid on the outside passage; salmon, shark, rock cod, and squid along the inside, with an occasional seal, porpoise, or sea bird for a change of diet. (Their name, "killer," is a man-word; it draws embarrassed attention from the most destructive of all killers, Civilized Man himself.)

The leading killer bull begins to echo-locate on the lone sperm whale and turns his pack toward a meal. Many a time they have torn to bloody bits the little piked whales of the Sound, and once they stopped a great gray whale in a running battle of two full hours in the view of excited campers on the beach. But never have they tackled a sperm, a stranger in their midst. While the killer bull hesitates, a rash member of his pack, teeth bared, darts toward the flank of the sperm.

44

OCTOBER

The sperm outweighs his attacker four to one and is skilled in fighting. He has sparred with rival males of his own kind in the mating season ten years in a row. He waits . . . and waits. Then, at the high strategic moment he twists his body in a fierce curve which brings his tail crashing against the killer. In the next motion he drops his jaw and swings it in a ten-foot slashing cut across the bull's soft underbelly. Between one breath and the next, the fight is over. A flabby, writhing strip of black and white, diffusing scarlet, rolls to the surface, as the killer lies in shock.

The distress cry of the wounded comrade is now uppermost in the mind of the pack; hunger is forgotten. They circle in confusion and one female tries to lift the dying animal. The sperm turns toward the west and the open sea. Not again will he venture within the still waters where his caution warned him *no!*

🐟🐟🐟

KILLER WHALES DESTROYED
VP-7 ACCOMPLISHES SPECIAL TASK.

I saw this puzzling story in *Naval Aviation News.* "Another successful mission against killer whales off the coast . . . destroys hundreds of killer whales with machine guns, rockets, and depth charges."

Alas, poor whales, and alas, poor Navy Captain Sherrill! Don't you know that each whale removed leaves a fleeting niche which nature soon will fill? Bombs away, sir. Your men will have their fun, and you your neat report of mission accomplished (signed) CINCNAFI/VP-7.

We humans like to classify wild animals as "good" or "bad." By labeling them, we fit them neatly into an arrangement; we bring a degree of order to a natural world that seems at times unorganized and frightening. We pass quick judgment on the rat; we call him "vicious, filthy, sly"—and we avoid the burden of understanding his life.

Man's attitude toward the killer whale is changing since we have been able to watch the behavior of individuals in captivity. Now we see a man riding on a killer's back in a pool, and scrubbing his back with a long-handled brush, and shaking "hands," and finally putting his head in the mouth of the "bloodthirsty beast."

No book about whales used to be complete unless it retold the threadbare story of Professor Eschricht's dissection of the stomach of a killer whale. I quote from the best of such books: "[He] discovered no less than thirteen complete porpoises and fourteen seals in the first chamber of its stomach. . . . A fifteenth seal was found in the animal's throat."

When I turn to the professor's original report, written in 1862, however, I find that this impressive meal was in fact only fragments of skin and bones, representing animals eaten by the killer over an unknown period of time. Yet I have no illusion that I have killed the story, for it is a good story, and good stories never die.

NOVEMBER

As the Little Calf tumbles at the surface on the first day
of November he sees at the rim of vision a dark speck on the
flat of the sea. Too distant for him to identify, it might be the
floating stump of a tree . . . the bloated carcass of a seal
. . . a wooden crate thrown from the deck of a passing ship
. . . perhaps a plastic jug—one of a million jugs, cast-off bits
of garbage impervious to water and corrosive salt, jetsam

blown by all the winds to the remote beaches of all the seas.

At his next lazy roll the dark blur suddenly grows. The Little Calf is alert. There is danger in the air. His mother changes course and moves away with all deliberate speed, along with others in the group. They breathe in measured tempo, senses sharp and voices low.

In an instant the dark thing is upon them and the family breaks in panic. A heavy, sea going tug, with "LIFE ARENA" blazoned across her bow, approaches in a churn of power. On the low peak there crouches a mysterious metal monster like a pair of giant tongs. A man stands in the crow's nest, muffled in wool against the gray chill of the day. He waves his arm madly and points to the left. Men in yellow slickers run on the afterdeck, carrying lines and tackle. The ship turns, heeling in a boil of foam while the men hang to the rigging.

The ship is chasing a small whale, a suckling female born the year before, another half-sister of the Little Calf. Back and forth the ship pursues her prey like a beagle on track of a hare. Now she pauses while the lookout tries to guess where the whale will blow, now surges ahead with smoke streaming from her stack. The whale tries to catch her sobbing breath but the dark thing is again on her all too soon.

A gunfire blast from the bow—a bright flash—a puff! The monster leaps. The tongs of stainless steel padded with foam rubber clasp firmly round the tapering body of the whale. Another *crack* and a small projectile charge of tranquilizing drug speeds into the flesh of the struggling animal. The ship backs off with a clang of bells. A nylon line stretches taut to the whale, dripping along its length and trembling like a fiddle string.

Now the waiting crew on deck slash the ropes that hold another odd contraption—a great white tub, part boat, part sled, a shallow trough, twenty feet long, of foam rubber reinforced with steel. It splashes to the sea and four men jump aboard, trained for the act. Frantically they pull it into place in front of the tug and directly aft of the whale.

The captain, though he stands in a chill wind, is drenched with sudden sweat. Never before in history have men taken a sperm whale alive. Will he be first? Will the line foul his propellers or break his rudder? Will the whale turn in anger on the sea-sled and smash his men?

He jerks his head and spits a brown quid over the rail, downwind.

The whale is growing quiet. She breathes heavily, with a deep "*Wh-oo-OOF!*" Was the dose of drug too large?

The script for this climactic scene was worked out weeks before in an atmosphere of endless talk, cigarettes, and coffee. Veterinarians, mechanics, instrument men, biologists, and old-time sailors were all consulted.

The men bring the sea-sled quickly to a point beneath the whale where the black flukes rise awkwardly from the water in the grasp of the metal tongs.

"Make it snappy!" shouts the captain. "I don't like her looks." In life jackets the men leap from the sled into the cold sea. The tug retreats, sliding the whale gently to her bed without a hitch. It is all over.

"By God, we've done it!"

The tug moves slowly astern to keep the nylon line taut. The swimming men hook dangling cables to steel eyes at either end of the sled. The captain signals: "Haul away!" and the great sled with its living load rises from the water. The boom leans perilously over the side; the deck slants; a bucket bangs against the rail. Now a man jerks a slender trip-wire following the line from deck to whale. The tongs spring open, and the whale lies free under the sky, passive, dumb, eyes rolling—a creature pulled against her will into the world of men. She is lowered at last to a cradle on the afterdeck, and a soft girdle of canvas and foam rubber is lashed across her body, pinning her flippers to her chest.

A yellow sun breaks through the overcast. The ship turns north-by-east, three-quarters east, full speed ahead. The radio alerts the owners of Life Arena on the mainland. The sailors change to dry clothing and stand in a quiet circle around the whale, seeing the slowly heaving sides, the tiny buglike creatures moving in confusion on the drying skin, the trembling flipper, the shining eye. Warm-blooded beast and warm-blooded men are translocated in time to a common level—a common stem of life two hundred million years ago.

The cook emerges from the galley, wiping hands on apron, pushing white cap over ear. "Chow's on!" With stony glance he passes the whale. "Whales and porpoises are a sailor's friends," he mutters, as he retreats to the warm comfort of his little kingdom above the fragrant stove. A religious man, in his way.

NOVEMBER

Now the animal trainer and the veterinarian discuss in worried tones a long red cut across the snout of the whale where she threw herself against a cable. They look at the blisters on her dome.

On through the starry night the ship forges ahead. At break of light the men are out on deck again staring at the whale. She is breathing a little easier, and she lunges now and then against her girdle. The vet smears a white ointment on the blisters. "It's just a sunburn, I think; one hour yesterday was enough to do it!" He rubs an antiseptic cream into the cut. He calls for a man to stand by full time with a cold salt-water spray to keep the tender skin as moist as nature requires.

At two in the afternoon the ship arrives at port; the captive whale is hoisted on a waiting flatbed truck. Reporters from the local press flash their lamps and scribble with thick pencils. An hour later, she is lowered into her final home, a pool of clean, circulating sea water in the aquarium.

The news has traveled quickly; scientists from New York, San Francisco, New Orleans, and Los Angeles are preparing to come and view, at close quarters, a real live sperm whale.

Meanwhile, the worried men of the Life Arena organization try to figure out a food regimen for the little whale. What does a toothless yearling eat? Has she been weaned already?

"At the start," says an old-time keeper, "give her castor oil." Saved from this indignity by the gentler advice of the vet, she is started off on a bland diet. Raw clams, mackerel, cod-liver oil, and vitamins, all blended creamy white and force-fed through a soft tube, are pumped into her stomach.

The formula works. Two gallons go down smoothly on the first try and four on the next. Don't reckon the cost—the whale is showing life. She circles actively, gives all the little signs that seem to say, Okay, all's well.

Three hundred miles away a mother searches for her young. . . .

In mid-November the ocean seldom rests. The black waves hurry southward, ever southward, in the fitful moving cloud shadows of the night. The wind moans softly to itself. To those who love the sea it is a peaceful time, a quiet time. They hear the humming of the universe. When now the music stops, the rolling sea keeps up the beat, the harmony goes on, and in the quiet dawn the sky flames red-grape purple, painted by the dust motes from a volcano's birth ten thousand miles away.

Newcomers, strange to him, are beginning to join the Little Calf's group, the first arriving bulls from the northland. They are in splendid shape; each has put on nearly a ton of pure fat every month during the summer feast among the Aleutian Islands.

At the same time, other bulls are leaving the group and moving south. They are few in number and do not really belong to the group. They live in waters of the southern hemisphere, straying to Mexico only when chance directs their course. In the south it is springtime. Soon the sun will shine there night and day.

The southbound whales are in search of food, the teeming fish life in waters little known to man. The whales move on to

NOVEMBER

Sixty South and still beyond to the edge of broken ice: enormous blocks of white a mile across, palaces, crystal vaults all blue-green, deep with mystery, the water dashing in and out, the moaning of the ice wells, the sudden roll and crash of melting spires. The fragment children of the Great White Continent, the Land of Silence, slide sighing from the mother lode and drift off, to erode, and corrode, and dissolve, and slop away to nothing at all in the Humboldt Current.

(Once I went to the South Pole and beyond, to suck my frozen breath at thirty-five below in midsummer, on the top of the icecap. A vast continent, greater than the whole of Europe and all so clean and quiet—there one can live, for a time at least, on pure emotion.)

〰〰〰

THE forerunners of whales have been traced in the fossil record to the beginning of the Age of Mammals, at which level in the rock the picture blurs, not only for primitive whales but for other mammals as well. Deeper and deeper in the rocks the mammals are fewer and smaller, down to rat-sized creatures that once fed on the leathery eggs of the dinosaurs. The links between whales and their dry-land ancestors are still entirely missing.

The student of animal evolution has three ways to unlock the mysteries of the past. He can study the fossil record, or the structure of living animals, or the associates of the animals.

Zoologists are said to be in love with dry bones. But every bone, large or small, is a memorial of the long history of its owner. It is a reflection of the present needs of the animal. (Artists, too, see beauty in bones, and respond to their message of function and fulfilled need.)

It would be useless, though, to study the skeletons of whales long gone if we did not also study the forms of living ones and try to understand their structure in terms of swimming, diving, food-gathering, and breeding.

Let us start with life in the womb, or the embryology of whales. Though whales are the strangest of all mammals—the farthest out from the mainstream of mammal life—the most highly modified—they have no structures fundamentally *new* but only familiar ones reworked. They have the same familiar parts as dogs and cats and cows and other mammals of the land. This is why zoologists are sure that whales developed from land mammals and not, say, from marine reptiles.

When the embryonic whale is only a pink blob an inch long, a pair of fleshy pimples sprout briefly on its loins, only to disappear as the little creature grows in size. Since these are precisely where the hind legs of a land mammal ought to be, they are surely a throwback to ancestral structures. They are as useless as nipples on a man. They illustrate how slow is the machinery of natural selection in the absence of pressures either *for* or *against* the survival of a part.

Now and then in the dull records of a whaling station there is an entry that could scarcely be credited, were it not supported by photographs or sketches. A whale with primitive, half-formed *hind legs* protruding from its body is brought to the whaling deck. How vanishingly small are the odds of a gene persisting through millions of years; inactive, yet suddenly able to quicken the embryo of a whale and to resurrect hind legs? Freak legs are always imperfect, of course, though those of a humpback whale killed near Vancouver stuck out more than a yard from the belly. They were symmetrical, and they included separate bones or cartilages that could be identified as the standard parts of legs.

In the fetus of every finback whale, tooth germs bud in the fleshy gums; they harden but never erupt to the surface. When the fetus has reached a length of thirteen feet they disappear without trace. The newborn finback has no teeth at all, but instead a massive apparatus of "baleen plates" which serve to filter plankton food from the sea. Baleen is a horny substance like fingernails.

For a while in embryonic life some porpoises have eight nipples, although no adult porpoise has more than two. Again, this must be a throwback to a dim past when the protowhale fed a litter of young on land.

So much for fossils and embryos. Another clue to the nature of ancestral whales is the comparative biology of modern species. Here the evidence is skimpy, for whales have been so long at sea and have accommodated so well to their watery world that they show few traces, in adult life at least, of their kinship to land forms.

The modern cetaceans are divisible into two families: the toothed whales and the baleen whales. The toothed whales are active predators, gobbling up food from the size of a sardine to the size of a one-ton squid. They adapt to many habitats. Some even live the year around in freshwater lakes of China. Each in his own habitat or ecologic niche, they are now split into seventy species. The baleen whales, on the other hand, include only ten species, all of them plankton feeders in the open sea.

The toothed whales have a single blowhole and a lop-sided skull; the baleen whales have a double blowhole and a symmetrical skull. The stomach in toothed whales is divided into three chambers or more; in baleen whales only three.

These and many other differences separate the two families and suggest that they had separate origins. In early Cretaceous time, more than a hundred million years ago, two stocks of small, hairy, warm-blooded animals lived in shallow brackish swamps near the sea. One was related to ancestral bears, dogs, and otters; the other to ancestral cows. Independently each stock went to sea, perhaps millions of years in time apart. Today we lump them together as "whales" because they have grown to look alike as a result of living together in a common ocean. Their evolution has been convergent.

An imperfect clue to the relationship of whales is the special load of parasites and fellow travelers that each carries in, or on, its body. All whales have stomach worms. When a kind of whale and a kind of worm have formed a long and harmonious (albeit one-sided) association, and when the whale subsequently evolves in response to a changing environment, the worm, too, is apt to deviate slightly from other worms of its clan.

The "fellow travelers" are such organisms as the diatoms that grow in slimy patches on the skin of whales. Some strains are known on whales of the northern hemisphere and others on whales of the southern, indicating that the two stocks of whales move in separate circles, each in its own half of the world.

Today exciting new theories are popping up to explain both the pace and the triggering forces of evolution. One theory holds that changes in the oxygen content of the atmosphere have been abrupt, rather than gradual. At each change, new plants and animals emerged while others faded away. Another theory says that declines in the earth's magnetic field from time to time allowed powerful cosmic rays to flood the surface with great intensity, producing mutations. Only the deep-sea organisms, covered by miles of water, escaped the cosmic blasts. Witness the living fossil, the coelacanth, which was hauled to the surface by an astonished African in 1938.

To sum up the history of whales, primitive whales are known from remains in rocky beds sixty to twenty million years old. Toothed whales are almost as ancient, from fifty million years to the present. Baleen whales are the youngest, from forty million years. The latest common ancestor lived a hundred million years ago. Perhaps his bones will some day be found in a chalk bed along with the remains of flying reptiles and sea birds with teeth.

〜〜〜

THE all-surrounding protean world of the Little Calf is filled with a hundred chemicals and a million living sparks and a billion bits of drift, no two alike. It is an endless, moving, thin, transparent soup; a cosmic stock forever old and ever new.

In this pale and swirling broth the Little Calf and his companions play at times with toys that bring them pain. They are forced to glimpse the rougher side of life.

The Year of the Whale

Of late, the Little Calf has tried to snatch remains of fish, the partly chewed debris squirting from the corners of his mother's mouth with each tremendous chomp. This is good, for it teaches him to grasp and tear, to twist and dart and seize the swimmers of the sea. But it is also bad, for now and then a fish is poisonous or bears choking spines or ragged scales. Some fish feed in transit through the deadly "red tides" and hold the poison in their bodies for a while.

A red tide is a living broth of simple cells, neither plant nor animal, but something in between. They contain green organs like a plant, and reddish blobs of pigment, and they propel themselves through the sea by whips as do certain primitive animals. (Must every living thing be plant or animal? It is man that makes the definitions.) These cells are called "dinoflagellates" and they can multiply with amazing rapidity. No one knows why. Among them are species which contain a fearful toxin, perhaps more lethal than botulinus toxin—and perhaps the most lethal toxin on earth.

The stomach of the Little Calf is not yet adjusted to foreign foods, and in his bloodstream the agents of immunity are only slowly building up. The lining of his throat is soft and smooth.

So today he has a bellyache. He slams his anvil head against mother's great side and rubs his corrugated back across her belly. She, source of all blessings, is, somehow, dimly back of all this pain. He thinks he is hungry and he nurses for a while, but spits up the milk in a spasm of distress, a gallon at a time.

NOVEMBER

The curdled creamy stuff rides in a floating trail behind, while phalaropes in flight break pattern in a quick, ruptive flash of silver and drop daintily to pick the bits.

The mother slides along without concern. This Little Calf is her twelfth (not counting two who never saw the light). She seems to know that their troubles come and go, though probably she does not remember the day some fifty years ago when she herself was playing off the Christmas Reef with a floating ball—in fact a coconut—that brought her grief. She swallowed it in fun and barely got it down. For a week it churned in her lower regions, now stopping the normal flow of food, now letting it by, till nature finally had her way and passed it on.

The mother learned a lesson from her pain. The North Pacific Ocean of today is strewn with nets in which are woven giant balls of green or browny glass, some eighteen inches through. They bear the signatures of shops in China, Korea, Japan, the Soviet Union, Canada, the U.S.A. and Mexico—the homelands of the fishing fleets. The glassy floats break free in storm and circulate to the playgrounds of the whales. Now and then a float disappears into the maw of a whale—but not that of an old whale with watchful eyes.

It is the twentieth of November and the middle of night. A hunter's moon illuminates the world of the Little Calf. The inner pangs of yesterweek are gone and their memory as well. He is content.

The flat molten silver of the sea swells at a point and bursts. Before the Little Calf can grasp the scene, an explosion of shapes appears at the point of rupture. A glistening black monster emerges on his back, thrashing tail at one end and gaping, upturned mouth at the other. In and around his lips, clawing and crawling and dripping, is a loathsome thicket of living limbs. The harem bull is locked in deadly combat with a squid.

Brief moments ago the squid was hunting near the surface, drawn by the light of the moon. He was a moving gray-pink ghost—a vast membrane streaming through a void, a silent flapping of vanes, a soft blur of naked whips. Then suddenly he was a tormented life fleeing in the dark.

The water stills, and the Little Calf slips along at a safe distance of a hundred yards behind the bull. Here nectar lingers in the wake and juicy morsels twist enchantingly to tempt his tongue. Some of them he follows down, and farther down. Now he reaches levels new and strange, where his muscles press and his tendons creak and his guts rumble and he feels for the first time the tingling tenseness of the masters of the deep.

Many miles away by now, among the bulls headed for the antarctic spring, is one who is also diving deep, very, very deep indeed. Chance has brought him to the one place in a thousand where the Ecuadorian cable hangs in a low loop between two submarine peaks, a half-mile down. The first report to reach his consciousness is familiar: Here is a slimy, tenuous, softly resistant thing—a squid no doubt, or food at least. He grasps the thing with lower jaw and gently pulls. It gives, but then with sudden snap it jerks his body round and seizes flipper in fatal coil of steel. He lunges in fright, twists his rubber mass to a shape most unlike a whale and lunges on. A new coil drops around his belly, another around his tail. His lungs flame in agony; sudden stars drift in shoals across his inner vision; a velvet curtain falls. . . .

His is an unrecorded death, for the cable does not break. The soft words flow around his grave; the messages of life and death, the loving words and stupid words, and pesos up and pesos down, and *"cuanto vale mas?"* The luminescent beasts and the dark beasts and the beasts in-between come to rob his tomb and tear the softening bits from his white frame. And the frame, too, unlocks in time, drops to the ocean floor and enters the geologic book, and the pages are closed.

ЯЯЯ

SOME years ago, near an island off the California coast, two bold men, a mathematician-engineer and a reporter, tested out a new device. Families and friends waited on the beach. In a diving bell the two sank by stages to the ocean floor. They breathed a foreign air, a mixture of helium and oxygen pumped from above. This they hoped would prevent the "bends," the agonizing needles in the flesh of divers sent too deep and brought too soon aloft. Down they went to pressures penetrating, killing. Then the bell was hoisted. One man was dying; the other woke to tell the story. They had gone

one thousand feet below—the greatest depth attained by men without protective diving suits.

ᔕᔕᔕ

IN his first year of life, as well as in the years to come, the Little Calf will see and hear a multitude of ships: the stinking, rackety little troller with one man at the lines; the purse seiner piled high with pungent, kelpy nets; the proud white tuna clipper, queen of the fishing fleet, a million dollars in her frame; the pleasure liner moving south to spice islands, her yellow lights reflecting on the dark pool of the sea, quick laughter from her rail. All these and many other craft the Little Calf will come to know.

But on the last day of November he sees one the like of which he will not see again. The captain of the thing he sees is very sure that once the trip is done, he will never again venture on the open waters of the North Pacific in a vessel of this kind.

The strange vessel is the *Search*, a unique experimental motor ship on her maiden run. A dozen scientists collaborated on her working plans. To a seafaring man she is a monster; a floating workshop crammed with awkward racks for water-sampling bottles, plankton nets and mud-grabs, fishing lines, fathometer, radar, direction-finder, stills and swivels, shackles, pots and pans. When the captain came aboard, he looked around the cluttered deck and rubbed his chin. "Well, I hope the weather holds," he said.

Now the *Search* is two days out of San Francisco with a motley crew. Biologists, physicists, chemists, a deck hand or two, an engineer, a cook, a mate, and Captain Larsen, whose quiet voice and easy smile relieve the tensions mounting in the crew.

On the second night the ship drifts off the Channel Islands under a small sail that holds her steady on the mild sea. The men rig a flood lamp. It hangs from a boom and dips below the surface of the water, spreading a yellow circle of light. The fishery biologist waits with a dip net—a funnel of nylon webbing fastened to a bamboo pole. He knows that darkness can bring strange reversals in the order of life in the sea. Some topside fishes go below, while other fishes, squids, and smaller organisms seek the upper levels. The reasons are obscure, though food must surely play a part, and escape from enemies, too. The water, clear in daylight, is now filled with pale, gauzy particles, some drifting, some jerking along on small invisible tracks, destined to live no more than an hour.

From the black margin of the pool of light a squid comes into view, pumping his jet stream in splendid rhythmic bursts of power, and close behind a great blur of white which suddenly snaps into focus as a California sea lion. As though warmed by the laughter of a crowd and the spotlight of a theater, the handsome beast turns and dives in sensuous loops. The broad flippers flare and fold and curve into art forms molded by the quick pressures of the sea. He folds them at his sides and shoots into the dark, long neck outstretched, a trail of silver bubbles streaming from nose and fur. Back again in the glare he hangs head down, relaxed, limbs weaving idly in the current—a weightless mass. The spotlight catches an eye and flashes back greenish-gold.

The man at the dip net calls in excitement, but the clatter of feet on deck alarms the virtuoso and he disappears. Within minutes, he is a mile away.

The following night the *Search* is far at sea, stopping on the hour to draw a water sample for the drowsy chemist huddled on the boat deck with his back pressed gratefully to the warm funnel from the engine room. Two zoologists play gin in the galley. Lulled at last by the throb of the diesels they stretch out, snoring, on a leather-covered bench. The mindless automatic pilot turns the wheel. The mate smokes thoughtfully on the bridge. The glass is dropping still; it's down to 29; he makes another entry in the log. A storm is coming, that's for sure.

The day breaks calm but the sky is troubled. Across its great vault ribbon streamers run from north to south, all blood-red. The captain reads the log and knows the signs; he orders to turn about for home. Within an hour the wind begins to keen, the rain beats down, the ship begins to rise and plunge.

A young biologist crouches by the lifeboat and hooks his legs around a towing bitt. He holds a telephoto lens, protected by a whipping plastic sheet. A camera fan, he is loving every wild moment. He sees the Little Calf a hundred yards away in a group of six. What a scene for *Life!* The storm is getting under way; far worse is yet to come. The whales are spaced precisely, two and two. They lift together in the swell and he sees the black, flaring nostrils in a quick-shutter scene against the wildness of the dimming light. Each whale is a rolling shadow on the slanting sea, each in a misty, moving frame of white. A rain squall slashes across the frame and shuts it off. The gloom is growing deeper.

Why is my tongue so thick? the young man wonders, and then he knows. Shoving precious camera under coat he lets the plastic sheet go down the wind and lurches off below, pausing for a wretched moment at the rail. In the dim, smelly cabin he finds the other savants laid in rows. The playing cards and magazines slide on the floor. The sickish fumes of diesel fuel rise from the shaft alley. (Something is loose below.) Damp garments swing in unison from ceiling hooks, dancing to the broken syncopation of gurgle and *thump!* The room turns green on the left as the deadlights plunge beneath the sea, then green on the right, then green on the left. . . .

A thunderous *boom!* The ship hangs in space; the deck tilts sharply; from the vacant lab comes a muffled crash and a cascade of broken glass.

The captain and mate brace their shoulders in a crowded locker and spin a hasty web of canvas and rope: a sea anchor. In a half hour it trails astern and the *Search* finds her head in the storm. She wallows less but plunges more. The rhythm of her engine stays at DEAD SLOW AHEAD. She waits a day and night, and still another day.

Black witches in tattered dress fly past the window of the

bridge. Goony birds, perhaps; they are gone before they show.

The Little Calf rises briefly from an underworld of quiet gray to a screaming wilderness of sound and motion—to the slashing fury of a Force Eleven gale. He is hungry, but his mother wants to stay below.

On the *Search* the men toss in their bunks, shivering, though the room is warm. Gray faces flop against gray pillows in the gloom. A voice cries from a troubled dream. A figure rises, leans on a slanting wall, then slowly moves to another cabin. Sweat trickles down the walls in the fetid atmosphere —no one sees or cares. The clock strikes out the watch: BONG BONG!

Another *crash!* There goes the lifeboat through the rail. The vessel trembles. Torrential streams fall from her upper deck, and her lower deck, and now she floats.

The storm loosens its grip as the low blue hills of the Golden Gate begin to loom. They seem to lie forever there; they will not come nearer. Now the death-pale faces begin to quicken. Here's the lee of the Farallons, and then the Gate itself. Everyone is on deck—a babel of talk—the grateful smell of toast and coffee and tomato soup and orange juice. (No onions yet, or frying bacon, if you please.)

So it goes, at times, when men of science try to penetrate the mother ocean, to pry into the lives of whales and seals and plankton; to measure isotopes, and phosphates, and wave dynamics. The ocean plays no favorites.

DECEMBER

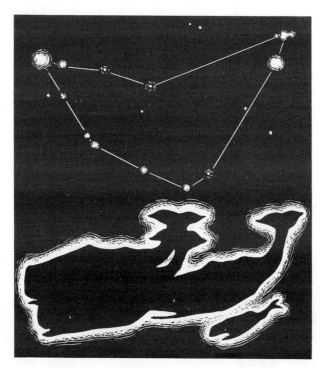

NOW it is December of the year of the whale. An early
blizzard whitens the seacoast from Alaska to the border of California and powders the tips of the towering redwoods at
Eureka.

A week of violent wind beyond Queen Charlotte Sound
drives the Dall porpoises into quiet reaches where they rest
awhile and taste the pungent cedar smoke of Indian fires.

The Year of the Whale

The Fur Seal Islands of the Bering Sea are deserted, bare and brown. The dry sea grasses whip against the sand and the red-and-orange lichens burn dimly in the frozen mist. The fur seal pups born this year stream south through the Aleutian passes, uncertain, pioneering, heading south to spend a year at sea. They meet for the first time the challenge of a North Pacific storm. They cannot feed. They cannot sleep. The weaker ones are doomed to die. Their silvery bodies drift by the hundreds to the shore, to wash and tumble in the tides and turn to dirty dishrags in the sand.

Fast ice forms in the Arctic Ocean. It forms along the northern rim of the Bering Sea where the gray whales have been feeding since July. Now they turn with steady purpose to the south, swimming a hundred miles a day. Their goal is Mexico. There, in shallow salt lagoons hidden from human eyes, they will bring forth their young and mate again. The last of their kind, the gray whales were saved in my lifetime by rigid hunting laws. Once a nearly vanished race, their numbers now are swelling. Each year in December when they pass in review below the cliffs of San Diego a hundred thousand people come to watch, and others drift in pleasure launches in their path. Nowhere else in the world are so many whales seen by so many people. No other kind of whale circles each year on so long a migratory route. No other kind of whale comes inland to breed.

Whalebirds, shearwaters, muttonbirds—the same by any name—have deserted the northern passes where they flocked by the millions in September and where they crossed

the tide rips and tore the white walls of mist. Now, after a jour-
ney of seven thousand miles, they are settled on barren islands
off Tasmania and are laying their eggs.

Still feeding along the coast of Mexico, the Little Calf and
his family feel the drop in temperature of the current flowing
from the east and north. They move by easy stages southward
to another stream, a warmer stream. The older whales,
cloaked in thick blubber, are not concerned with cold: they
are in fact often too warm. The youngsters, though, prefer the
milder areas.

During the long impersonal course of evolution those
mothers who by chance remained nearest the equator, and yet
in pastures rich in food, were most successful in their motherhood. Their young survived. The chance became the habit;
the chance assumed "survival value."

In the bodies of the newly adult males, ten years of age or
more, new urges start to prick, new itchings flow and ebb (but
spring is still three months away). They nose around the female whales, restless and disturbed. Repulsed, they wander
off to feed and play. Some travel on . . . and on. . . . They
reach Korea and the islands of the Kurile Chain. They pass the
junks and sampans—the *skimbo sens*, the small and valiant
ships of the Orient. They rub against new fellows of their kind,
but yet not kin; their voices somewhat strange; their blood-
lines surely similar, but alien.

The mother of the Little Calf is hungry. Too long she has
dozed in the winter sun, only inches under the surface of the

sea. She sighs. She draws a dozen deep drafts of air and then she turns below. Her tail flashes against the blue. She does not sink, she undulates, she presses firmly down. Her heartbeat drops to ten per minute, barely thumping, slow, pumping five gallons at a stroke. The blood retreats from limbs and skin and tail; it keeps alive the massive brain and heart. The red-black muscles of her flesh begin to pour their hidden stores of oxygen into her veins.

Now the massive beds of fat begin to serve. Their spongy, oily cells relax and offer up their air. The pressure grows. She continues down. Her body goes in debt for oxygen, but not for long. A trillion cells suspend, they tolerate, they hold. For half an hour she feeds and then she pushes to the top to breathe. Her lungs are clean and fresh; their walls are thin. In sweet abandon she sucks the upper air all pure and unpolluted. Her breath is a rustling sound like a surf on a smooth beach—a soft sighing in the music of the wind. It is a sound like no other on the sea. She has fed two thousand feet below and yet survives.

𝕤𝕤𝕤

I sometimes wonder why it is that, when a pregnant whale dives, and the fetus in her womb begins to feel the awful weight and the slowing pulse, the little thing is not expelled like a popping cork. Perhaps, when the oxygen level drops, it too begins to "dive" in its own small way, to obey the automatic signals in her blood.

DECEMBER

The mother sperm whale swims along day after day in a repetitious world, a primal, simple, fluid, unsophisticated world. Dawn and bright noon and dusk, and dark, and moon, and then another dawn. A looming of clouds, a rain squall, a wind, a whisper of sleet on her back, a calm, a flowing wetness, then clear skies again.

"The swimming speed of whales is impossible," the scientists were wont to say. "By all the laws of physics their energy cannot be sustained." The men pushed wooden models through water courses and clocked the forces entertained. The movement of the whales was still beyond belief. So they made a rubber-plastic whale, a simulated whale with rippling skin—a warm, vibrating counterpart of life. That worked. The motion of its outer surface was the clue: a soft accommodating to the waves, a lack of turbulence; efficiency at peak.

And the sperm whales continue to move at speeds unrealized by man. Through a strong sculling motion of their flukes and a total, compensating motion of their trunks they surge ahead—at twenty knots in panic, under six at ease. Their spouts of air emerge as geysers from the placid sea. They glide along in solitary dignity, then join in lines like cavalry horses of old. They leap, descend, rise, and spout together in joyous mood, easy, regular, majestic. How wonderful are these beasts akin to man.

A great deal of water has flowed through the life of the Little Calf—necessarily so, as the whale and the water are one. But do whales drink? I search the literature of science for the answer. Perhaps the question is one that should not be asked. Perhaps a beast immersed in water all his life cannot help drinking. But this is a glib answer.

Whales are never thirsty, since all their food is wet and

all the air they breathe is damp. And, too, their chemistry is such that much of the fat they eat is turned, or cold-burned, to water in their gut. It is fair to say that they do not drink in the deliberate sense. They do not open their mouths to imbibe sea water. Yet surely, as they feed, great drafts of water must sluice into their throats, pushed by the pressure of the sea.

At the core of the matter is the fact that sea water is three or four times saltier than whale blood. Their kidneys are constantly pumping uphill against osmotic force. For castaway men it is fatal to drink from the sea or in desperation to drink their own urine. Why is it different for whales?

The truth is that man is a queer animal, standing far apart from the nearest beast. We *must* ignore his frame of reference, his words and definitions, his willingness to think that other creatures act as he does.

In the laboratory, rats and mice and squirrels can live for many months on sea water and dry food alone. They lose weight at first and often fail to reproduce, but nonetheless they live. So it must be with whales. They must have great tolerance for salt, and what is called their salt elimination "problem" is in fact no problem at all. The main clue is derived from study of their kidneys—peculiar grapelike clusters in a common sheath; a thousand lobules, each a small kidney.

Perhaps another clue lies in the volume of their urine. This is not known. I can imagine a stainless-steel device, implanted around a whale's bladder duct, which bounces radar back and forth and sends a wireless signal to the scientists following by boat, spelling out the rate of flow throughout the day and night. Crazy? Maybe so.

In any case, whales do not drink as you and I do. They swallow salty water with their meals, though not from choice.

DECEMBER

They pass off the salt by methods not unlike our own and tolerate the burden while it lasts.

ᏒᏒᏒ

ONE morning, as the mother of the Little Calf lies at the surface with baby mouthing her breasts, he pulls away. What's wrong with the milk? It has a most unpleasant taste, a flavor not unknown but never quite so strong.

Over the surface of the sea an iridescent purple shimmer, moving from the east, is spreading around the pair. The mother feels it in her mouth and eyes and moves downwind to cleaner surroundings.

Beyond the horizon a ship is pumping out a slop tank, filled partly with oil and partly with rusty water. The smelly broth of pollution will float for many days, until the sunlight turns it into tarry balls and the currents carry the little balls to the beaches and the seas finally pound them into dark grains of gummy sand.

Brown pelicans and boobies settle to the ocean to rest and feed. The oil seeps into their plumage and slowly creeps around their sides as the downy feathers lose their buoyancy. When the birds take off at last and come to land they tremble in the wind; their skin is wet and cold. Dirt from the nesting ground clings to their oily breasts. They try to preen but only spread the mess.

The scene closes on dark, indefinite forms huddled in the drift, feebly moving, death not far away.

In mid-December the group that the Little Calf belongs to has wandered to a feeding ground at Twenty-two North, between the mainland of Mexico and the Islas Revillagigedo. For no special reason they are separated from the other harem group. In a few weeks the groups will join.

The Little Calf and his family linger here through the latter half of December, lazy and content. They have found a place where food is rich, where cold and warm currents meet and bring together a great variety of squids and fishes.

The harem bull has been here often. Now he dives for an hour and a quarter, as long as any sperm whale can hold his breath. Deep down, the white prow of his body is lit by the pale reflection of a noctilucent cloud containing things too small for him to see, each thing a single cell drifting in a self-perpetuating glow of beauty. He rises to the surface at last with three hundred pounds of new food pressing his stomach.

He knows by throbbing feel the peaks and canyons of the submarine mountain ranges; the oozy fans of silt sliding softly, unseen, over the black plains; the awesome cliffs and grottoes; the meandering rivers of brine coursing their ancient channels in the rock. He knows where the octopus hides and where it can be seized when it strays from the safety of its cave. He knows the shape of rotting treasure craft and the rusting hulls of modern ships of war, complete with small, particulate, rusting heaps of metal representing men.

DECEMBER

He and the other old-timers of his group have memorized the world below—at a certain cost to their handsome bodies, to be sure. They carry the scars of contact with hidden rocks: teeth chipped and broken, foreheads scarred and furrowed. In the world around them—their biosphere—lies their greatest peril.

We humans here on land tend to think that all wild creatures have important "enemies," in terms of larger, fiercer beasts that feed by habit on them. But what about the lion and the wolf? The grizzly bear? The shark and crocodile? From whom do *they* flee? From none, except while they are young or when they are beset by others of their own kind. Their enemies are the small, erosive, unimpressive costs of living: the storms and droughts, fires and floods, days of starvation, dangerous cliffs and treacherous bogs, thin ice, scratches, infections, tumors, lice and other biting bugs, roundworms and tapeworms, broken teeth and bones, poisonous foods, and all the thousand natural shocks that flesh is heir to. Death comes to them slowly, not as the quick extinction of a rabbit surprised at his nest by a fox. The king of beasts dies with a whimper in the dark thicket. And the great sperm whales die far at sea, their passing rarely known to man.

ᔕᔕᔕ

I SEE a kind of moon-earth relationship in the spacing of the individual whales and in the spacing of the harems; not too near and not too far. The gregarious instinct pulls them close, while the territorial instinct repels them, one from another. People are like this, of course. Our basic urge for privacy is balanced by our need to fraternize.

The origin of social use of space by whales and men is now a million years behind. We reconstruct it, though, in general terms of need. A case in point: each whale must feed. If it crowds too close it competes with its neighbor for fish; if it travels alone it fails to hear the signal when a lucky member of the group finds a food bonanza. If it travels apart it is more exposed to danger; in a group it shares protection.

Some would say that the rude exiling of young males by the harem bull has survival value for the sperm whale species; it prevents inbreeding. Among wild animals, though, I see no harm in mating-in-the-family. With nature constantly at work screening out the unfit through storm, disease, predation, and starvation, the finest stock will survive to breed, regardless of the parents' blood relationship.

Some years ago I shared an office at Cambridge University with Julian Taylor, a friendly chap who identified himself as a "dog physiologist." Over a cup of tea and a sausage roll he told me a strange tale. He had wintered on the Antarctic Peninsula. The sea ice froze that year like a wall around an isolated pool where two hundred whales were trapped. They could not escape to the open sea. Killer whales, little piked whales, and a beaked whale were locked in a prison fold. Back and forth they churned in despair, sloshing water against the ice walls, where it froze and penned them even more securely. Some poked their noses straight up in the air, and the men in the sledge party crawled on bellies, excited, to touch a living whale. Six months later, when the same party passed the pool, there were not more than twenty whales. The others had either starved or swum beneath the ice to safety forty miles away.

As a naturalist I write about the environment of whales, regarding nature for the moment as the world without man. But man is a part of nature, too; part of the surroundings of the whale. With terrible swiftness man has fouled the waters and the land and the air above. And far beyond the air he has shot magnetic needles to circle the earth and confuse the astronomers. His radioactive wastes flow from the majestic mouth of the Columbia to enter the bodies of whales, while other debris rains from the sky to enter the tundra moss, to be eaten by caribou and by lemming mice.

The wildest and cleanest of the oceanic islands—indeed the jewels of the sea—are bulldozed by men-trained-in-violence, while other islands shudder under the test shots of atomic bombs. "Why not? They're *uninhabited;* they're *not in use;* they're *unimproved,*" say these men in bewilderment.

How can the naturalist answer? What can the poet say? What new tongue can speak to the men who know and use only the language of force?

Says the black man Laurençot in *The Roots of Heaven:* "God, Schölscher, how can we talk of progress when we're destroying, all around us, life's most beautiful and noble manifestations? Our artists, our architects, our scientists, our poets, sweat blood to make life more beautiful, and at the same time we force our way into the last forests left to us, with our finger on the trigger of an automatic weapon, and we poison the oceans and the very air we breathe with our atomic devices. . . . We've got to resist this degradation. Are we no longer capable of respecting nature, or defending a living beauty that has no earning power, no utility, no object except to let itself be seen from time to time? . . . It's absolutely essential that man should manage to preserve something other than what helps to make soles for shoes or sewing machines, that he should leave a margin, a sanctuary, where some of life's beauty can take refuge and where he himself can feel safe from his own cleverness and folly. Only then will it be possible to begin talking of a civilization."

🌀🌀🌀

IN late December the Little Calf is beginning to wander more often from his mother's side. He watches with keen interest a group of six-year-olds at play; his older half-brothers. They have found a floating log ten feet long and as thick as a fence post; battered, soft to the touch, and festooned with greenish strands of seaweed. Long ago it tumbled down a Kamchatka river, followed the lazy North Pacific Drift, and is now moving along in waters off California. One of the young males takes the log in his mouth and whips it from side to side, growling in whale language, as if enjoying an imaginary conflict with a fearsome creature of the deep. What fun! What an exquisite feeling in his mouth, where chafing nubbins of teeth are slowly pushing upward to the surface of the gums—they will not reach the surface until he is nine years old.

His fellows see the action and move in on the target. One of them is struck by accident on his tender belly. Anger floods his brain. Transformed in a flash to a fighting bull he wheels away in a churning circle of foam, shoots back like a torpedo, and rams a startled companion. The community click-talk changes its tenor. The young whales, impelled by strange new feelings, arrange themselves like petals on a daisy, heads pointing toward the center, tails flung outward.

Then the wildness passes and again they tug happily at the log, flipping it from side to side.

⟡⟡⟡

CAN the behavior of the young whales really be called "playing"? Again I wonder at the meaning of a word. It slips easily from my pen, though I am not sure that it fits the behavior of a wild animal. Zoologists argue the point. One says flatly that animals do not work and therefore cannot be said to play. Another defines play as any behavior apparently performed for the sake of the activity itself rather than for any useful purpose. Still, the idea is widely accepted that animal play is a *young* activity; it is exploratory; it is practice for adult behavior.

I suppose that only men can truly play, or make love or wage war, or commit incest or suicide. By first definition these activities are human, though some biologists will write, for example, that otters play on a mud slide and that black ants war against red ants. Thus they write in a kind of biological shorthand to simplify the description of complex or obscure activities. I have no real objection to their doing so. When a distinguished ornithologist talks of "divorced" or "unemployed" penguins his meaning is clear enough. When I write of "idle" bulls on the fur-seal grounds of Alaska I pass no moral judgment.

Enough of definitions. I turn to the playful behavior of a dolphin relative of the Little Calf, who was called Opononi. She was named for a seashore village on the North Island of New Zealand and her short career was so delightful that I must digress for a moment to describe it. A boatowner in that village began to notice a young female dolphin who seemed to have no fear of people. She enjoyed them and gradually came so close inshore that she could be stroked, and finally ridden on, by swimmers. At Christmastide she was attracting two thousand visitors a day to Opononi Beach.

"She had an uncanny knack of finding out those who were gentle among her young admirers, and keeping away from the rougher elements," wrote Anthony Alpers. "Some people got so excited when they saw 'Opo' that they went into the water fully clothed just to touch her."

The New Zealand government passed a law to protect Opononi. On the same day she failed to appear. Her body was found in a coral pool nearby. The circumstances of her death are a mystery and no one is blamed.

"When word reached the village that the dolphin was dead, a gloom came over everyone. That evening as dusk settled over the harbour her body was towed by a small boat to the beach where she played so joyfully not long before. . . . Later, with reverence after their fashion [the Maori] buried her beside the Memorial Hall and covered her grave with flowers."

DECEMBER

ᔕᔕᔕ

THE Little Calf has now followed his mother and several other whales on a feeding trip to green water within sight of the Mexican coast. The harem bull was not aware of her going, nor would he have stopped her had he known; she is not in heat and therefore not attractive. Mother and calf are now wallowing in the midst of a peculiar stream of marine organisms, a vast, incredible Noah's Ark population of bony fishes, sharks, and squids; sea birds and seals; porpoises and whales. Birds by the thousands, wheeling, screaming, and diving, give evidence that the stream extends beneath the surface of the water for many miles. It is an amazing river of life.

Its smallest units are drifting specks, plants invisible to the naked eye, now multiplied to numbers beyond all reckoning. Two weeks ago, in an eddy current of the southeastern Pacific, the stage was set for their blooming. The environment was suddenly right for a population explosion, as it had not been for several years. The critical factors of protracted sunshine, upwelling of seawater heavy in nutrient chemicals, and drop in temperature combined to trigger the explosion. The animals now composing the stream of life have little in common except that all are gorging on creatures smaller than themselves, down to the microscopic crustaceans in the second link from the bottom who are feeding in myriad pink swarms upon the one-celled plants.

Several hundred sperm whales in migration have paused to enjoy the food riches, while others, including the Little Calf and his mother, have been drawn here from their wintering grounds. For one old bull the feast is a climax to a long life. He is now seventy-five years old and in poor health; he will not live through the winter. Another bull is younger, larger, and in better condition; he has reached his prime at age forty-four and will grow no more. His appetite is insatiable. Though he rests near the surface of the ocean for several hours in midday and feeds mainly at night, he stows away two tons of food every twenty-four hours. Squids and fishes of a dozen kinds go through his maw; he drives ahead blindly. When a bitten chunk of tuna falls from his mouth he swallows the rest and tarries not to retrieve the scrap. A length of fishline with six hooks, wound around the tail of a ten-foot shark, goes down his throat without a hitch. The furrows underneath his throat stretch to accommodate the mouthful, though his stomach pouch (one of four in a row) tries spasmodically and briefly to expel the mass. A young sea lion, far from his home in a rocky cave of Isla Cedros, is sleeping at the surface, glutted near to bursting. He awakens in alarm. His last image of the world is a cavernous whale mouth fringed with white, blurred in a rush of foam.

ഇഇഇ

THE teeth of the sperm whale are massive, each weighing a half-pound or more. Each one is creamy white, a cylinder lightly curved, a thing of art which fits delightfully into the palm of my hand. As my fingers rub one automatically, they feel the well-worn tip—the polished anvil of a thousand meals. Long scores on the root identify the peculiar marks of the socket, left imprinted on the growing tooth, as marks on a bullet identify the one rifle from whence it sped on its errand of death. Crisscrossed on the whale's tooth, and round and round, are ripple marks in ivory, each a memorial to feast or famine. One splendid gorging, a full fortnight long, on a school of sharks off Tiburon is recorded for life in the solid root of the tooth.

Should the prophet Jonah be included among the foods of the sperm whale? There are several strands to the answer. Those good people—and they number in the thousands—who believe that Jonah was indeed swallowed by a whale and cast up later alive will find reinforcement in an article in the *Princeton Theological Review*, in which Ambrose John Wilson of Oxford University argues that Jonah's captor was a sperm whale.

"Of course," he wrote, "the gastric juice would be extremely unpleasant but not deadly. [The whale] cannot digest living matter, otherwise it would digest the walls of its own stomach."

Wilson rests his argument on a pair of grim tales from whalemen.

A ship in the South Seas in 1771 had one of her boats bitten in two by a sperm whale. The beast seized one unlucky crew member in her mouth and went down with him. "On returning to the surface the whale ejected him on the wreckage of the broken boat, much bruised but not seriously injured."

A worse fate befell another victim in 1891.

The Year of the Whale

"The *Star of the East* was in the vicinity of the Falkland Islands and the lookout sighted a large Sperm Whale three miles away. Two boats were launched and in a short time one of the harpooners was enabled to spear the fish. The second boat attacked the whale but was upset by a lash of its tail and the men thrown into the sea, one man being drowned, and another, James Bartley, having disappeared, could not be found. The whale was killed and *in a few hours* was lying by the ship's side and the crew were busy with axes and spades removing the blubber. *They worked all day and part of the night.* Next morning they attached some tackle to the stomach which was hoisted on the deck. The sailors were startled by something in it which gave spasmodic signs of life, and inside was found the missing sailor doubled up and unconscious. He was laid on the deck and treated to a bath of sea water which soon revived him. . . . He remained two weeks a raving lunatic. . . . At the end of the third week he had entirely recovered from the shock and resumed his duties."

My friend and counselor in matters of cetology, Francis C. Fraser of the British Museum, wrote me on the subject:

"I am glad to have heard that in the most recent translation of the Old Testament the Jonah incident refers to a 'fish' and not a 'whale,' so that in future Jonah can be referred to the Fish Section [of the Museum]. *The Expository Times,* 1907, had a correspondence relating to Bartley and (this pleases me) includes a letter from the wife of the Captain of *Star of the East* contradicting the truthfulness of the story.

"Theologians," Fraser concludes, "should not question the omnipotence of the Lord but acknowledge the miraculous nature of the Jonah incident."

Another "swallowing" is reported by Egerton Y. Davis,

who was a surgeon with the harp-seal fleet out of Newfoundland in 1893. In 1947, as an old man, he wrote:

"One of the lads on another ship had the misfortune, in full view of his comrades, to become isolated from the others on an icepan, from which he fell into the icy waters in the proximity of a huge sperm whale. The whale was apparently as lost and out of season in those Arctic waters as he was confused and angered by the sudden appearance of a fleet of ships and men.

"Somehow the poor fellow was swallowed by the whale, which then made straight for one of the smaller sealers. A lucky shot from the small cannon mounted on her stern mortally wounded the huge mammal and served to change his course, though he traveled a full three miles out to sea before his death thrashing. The next day he was found floating belly-up by one of the longboats as it was searching for seals; and though it was impossible under those conditions to bring him in, the men, by a valiant effort and many hours of hard labor, were able to hack their way through his abdomen below the diaphragm and isolate his huge gas-filled 'upper stomach,' which apparently contained their comrade. This was severed with some difficulty at the cardia and in the first portion of the duodenum. They brought it to me for inspection and also for preservation of the man's body, as it was hoped he could be returned to his native Argentia (Newfoundland) for burial.

"At first I attempted the dissection with my scalpel but quickly gave it up in favor of one of the sharpest galley knives. The stomach was finally opened and gave off an overpowering stench. A fearsome sight met our eyes. The young man had apparently been badly crushed in the region of his chest, which may have been enough to kill him outright. (In any event an examination of his lungs revealed a general atelectasia with marked hemorrhage throughout.) The most striking findings were external, however; the whale's gastric mucosa had encased his body (particularly the exposed parts) like the foot of a huge snail. His face, hands, and one of his legs, where a trouser leg had been pulled up or torn, were badly macerated and partly digested. . . . It was my opinion that he had no consciousness of what happened to him. Curiously enough some lice on his head appeared to be alive."

Well and good, Dr. Davis, though it is strange that you waited more than half a century to tell your tale. Perhaps it will be confirmed some day through the discovery of the logbook of the schooner *Toulinguet*, or through the revival of some grisly sea chanty sung in the taverns of St. Johns. Meanwhile, may I venture to doubt it?

𝔖𝔖𝔖

WHILE the Little Calf is resting with his companions, disaster strikes another group of sperm whales on the strand of Perkins Island, in far-off Tasmania. (There's a saying among biologists that no wild animal ever dies of old age.) Thirty-seven bulls have moved southward from the tropics, forced out by more belligerent males, excluded for one season at least from the joys of harem life. It is summer in the Southern Ocean and the bulls are leading a straggling procession of displaced bachelors and battered old fellows toward the rich pastures of the sub-Antarctic seas. As the bulls turn a rocky headland of

DECEMBER

Perkins Island on a falling tide, in a brisk onshore wind, they suddenly panic. None has been here before. Strange, confusing echoes return from the reefs, the breakers, and the tide rips. They plunge wildly ahead, following the leader.

A week later a reporter for the *Queensland Witness* stands on the beach in a daze, recording the greatest known disaster of its kind among sperm whales. A thousand tons of black rotting meat are strewn about. Unsupported by water, the lumpish bodies have collapsed; the jaws gape tragically; dark oil oozes into the sand.

"What's your opinion?" the reporter finally asks a sun-burned fisherman who has walked from his shack two miles around the point. "Mass suicide?"

"Well, I was pulling my crayfish pots last Tuesday mid-day and she was blowing pretty hard when I begin to hear this kind of *moaning* or maybe *roaring*. It scared the hell out of me. I've lived here thirty years and never heard nothing like it. It kept on all afternoon and all night. By Wednesday morning it was gone. Jack, here"—pointing to a pal—"come down the coast and told me what it was all about. By then they was all dead. The way I figger it, the bull whales were hot after a cow and they forgot to check the tide."

Perhaps this explanation will serve. Whale scientists, though, will point to the fact that only toothed whales are known to run aground in groups, and only toothed whales depend strongly on echo-location. In unfamiliar, shallow waters, may not these social animals be confused by false echoes and perish in a mad stampede to follow the leader?

JANUARY

THE Little Calf's size is increasing daily. He nuzzles warmly at his mother and sucks. Each full, fat, satisfying meal leaves him replete. A thin plaque of ivory settles on the root of each tooth, a lasting metabolic product of the meal.

But what is he thinking? Is he fearful? What new, exciting images troop across his plastic mind? What new linkages (in neurologic terms) are forming in his brain? Does *color*, for example, strike his memory first, or *form?* Alas, how little we know—how little we can ever know. How little we can penetrate the mind of a creature left so far behind in the evolutionary attempt at a fuller life.

In early January the harem group begins to move north and west, raggedly, on an aimless course, a few miles a day. The Islas Revillagigedo drop below the skyline for another year.

When the Little Calf was born four months ago the family included sixteen cows; now there are fourteen. The mother of the yearling captured for Life Arena searched for her calf until the tension in her breasts eased away. By then she was far from the group. She traveled alone for a month in subtropic waters and joined at last a passing band of whales, largely strange, but including a few known to her from association in the past.

The sixteenth cow disappeared completely from the harem group. Her bloated carcass, a seven-month fetus within it, drifted to a rocky beach near Manzanillo, where the ravens and gulls and wild dogs and skunks feasted on the black meat for many weeks and after the flesh was gone feasted for another week on the blowfly pupae in the sand beneath it. Perhaps her pregnancy was one of the extremely rare type in which the fetus grows outside the womb and finally stops the normal flow of blood and pinches off the mother's life. Who can say? Her bones turned chalky white in the fierce Mexican sun, and once a turtle hunter, a beachcomber, found welcome shelter for the night by throwing his poncho across a pair of her long ribs.

On the twelfth of January the Little Calf's family overtakes a large group of sperm whales, two hundred or more. These are not unexpected, for they have been leaving a broad and well-marked trail of sensory clues: muffled smashing noises, low-pitched groans, clicks, and the creakings of rusty hinges—the fugue and plainsong of a wandering band, as well as clues that can be tasted: urine, pale diffusing clouds of yellow feces, and floating lumps of ambergris, a most peculiar body stuff.

Ambergris, a gray, waxy substance, grows in the large intestine of sperm whales and in no other species. Boulders of it up to nine hundred pounds in weight float on the sea. Its pungent, earthy odor is deceptive, for when purified in the laboratory it is transmuted to a perfume base worth ten dollars an ounce. "It always reminds me," says Christopher Ash, "of a cool English wood in spring, and the scent you smell when you tear up the moss to uncover the dark soil underneath."

In the trail of the whales are also visual clues to their passing: birds wheeling and diving to snatch at fragments of food, and sharks following to scavenge. These camp followers remain for a day or so and then wander off, while others take their places. A great white shark, thirty feet long, follows the group with interest for a week, but no crippled whales fall behind; the fearsome eater finally turns away. The whales pass a basking shark, the largest of all the fishes of temperate seas, forty-two feet in length. In spite of its sleepy name, it swims steadily near the surface with open mouth and goggle eyes, feeding and breathing in one efficient motion. Plankton masses cling in reddish gobs to its gill rakers until they finally pass deeper into its throat and disappear.

When the Little Calf is hungry he follows his mother's flank, no more than inches from her finely sculptured form. The great creation and the small creation move in silence as a double whale. A large swirl on the surface of the water cuts a smaller one; they both dissolve in an eddy of liquid lace and suddenly are gone. Low, bushy, vapor-columns linger in the air . . . then only sky and sea remain.

On the afternoon of the fifteenth of January the Little Calf is witness to a frightful scene: a full-scale battle between bulls. Though he will see the pattern repeated many times and will in fact participate when he matures, this is his first sight of the great beasts rolling and thundering in his path. The other whales of the family, the noncombatants, are disturbed by the sight and sound, for this is the first such encounter of the year. (The peak of the mating season is still a full three months away.) The old cows snort explosively. The young cows and the young bulls hover near the surface at the start of the struggle, trembling like sheep.

A young bull, fifteen years old, has been traveling with the group for several months. He has cut loose from a bachelor group—a timid group of young males coursing the road of the larger herd but a mile or so behind. During the past week he has fed in desultory fashion, coming often to the surface to cruise among the members of the harem group, cutting in and out among the females for hours on end. In passing, he has sparred briefly with other young males and has driven them away with the fierceness of his rushes. Yesterday he found himself near the forefront of the migrating band. In a sudden, blind instinctive surge he slammed his body against a full-grown bull. Incredibly, the bull gave way. The younger whale did not press his advantage but swam on. The impulse to fight was canceled by the quick submission of the foe.

Now in early afternoon of a bright, electric winter day he swims toward the father of the Little Calf who is outriding the harem two hundred yards to windward. A tension, a vast irritation, powers his muscular strokes. Nearing the great bull he rotates his flippers and bends his tail flukes upward. His snout rises from the surface on a long slant, until his eyes are clear of the surface.

The older bull has known for a full minute what was in store. The strong, familiar rasping signals of challenge assail his ears. Annoyed at first, he is now aroused. He reacts by rote to the threat. His broad tail, fourteen feet across, gleams in the sky as he dives to a depth of two hundred feet. He turns and shoots straight to the surface. His snout rises like a black barrel into the air, higher and higher still, until his dome is fifteen feet above the water. Here he hangs, with eyes peering into the open air, circling slowly, while his tail and flippers beat the water in strong sculling motions.

The young whale turns on his left side and charges, clapping his jaw violently, forcing each tooth with a smash into the firm white socket of the upper gum. The old bull turns deliberately on his back, belly up, responding in kind with a racket that carries through the sea for a league in all directions. His great jaw swings at right angles to his body, tip waving in air. The first impact of the bodies with a total mass of a hundred tons throws a geyser of green water high into the sky. Within seconds the movements of the whales are lost in a smother of foam. Each infuriated beast is trying to engage the other's jaw, or to seize a flipper—the action is all confused.

The pair sink into a maelstrom. They break apart and race in opposite directions. The tortured surface of the sea tosses like a riptide in a rocky channel.

They turn. They charge at full speed and collide in another mighty, tumbling interchange of power. Now the old bull is riding the back of the younger. His head is out of the water for twenty seconds—a black head marked with red blood and white furrows of blubber. Strangled, bellowing noises from nostrils and throats rise from the vortex of battle.

The third exhausting round is the last. The thrashing beasts, insensate, driven by will, not muscle, tumble into the path of the migrating herd. The other whales speed away in fright.

The jaw of the old bull is locked firmly with the jaw of the young one as the two bodies sink trembling below the surface of the sea in a final contest of power.

Suddenly the young male is done. Silent and dazed; he makes no further challenge, though the old bull tears and worries at his quiet form. The body of the young male is strangely awkward, oddly out of balance, as he swims away. One side of his jaw is broken; it will heal in time. Three ribs are fractured, too. As the blood drains cleanly from the bodies of the whales in the purifying sea, white scars in even, rakelike rows loom on the black skin.

The young male rallies at last and sinks horizontally, deeply, into the ocean, without lifting his tail. He swims a mile before he rises painfully to the surface and takes a solitary position at the rear of the herd. Long, slinky shadows circle his body for a while and then fade away. Blue sharks, attracted by blood, are frightened by the movement of his flippers.

In the confusion of battle, the Little Calf has followed his mother, or so he thinks. She is all at once strange. This is another whale! He starts in panic to search among the herd, all senses alert. But mother has gone below on a feeding trip, and not until the soft colors of evening have painted air and water alike is she reunited with her calf.

The harem bull keeps pace with the herd, though he suffers. Pain jerks at the base of his jaw. A throbbing fever sets in and dulls his senses for a week. He cannot lick his wounds. Held in the rubbery bindings of his own gigantic skin he is a victim of geologic time. He has learned nothing from the battle, nothing at all. He played his part faithfully, and according to the numbers, guided by an invisible coach.

JANUARY

♫♫♫

"My God! Mr. Chase, what is the matter?" I answered, "We have been stove by a whale!"

OWEN CHASE

A matter that has aroused the curiosity of every student of sperm-whale behavior is brought to mind by the fight between the bulls and by the use of their massive heads as battering rams against the foe. This is the record of whale attacks on ships and men.

The good ship *Union* was sent to the bottom in 1807, the *Essex* in 1820, the *Ann Alexander* in 1851, and the *Kathleen* in 1902. These are some of the stout little hulls, splintered and sunk under attack, whose names are now immortalized in whaling literature. As recently as 1963 a sperm whale smashed a fishing launch off Sydney, killing a man.

The great fighting whale that sank the *Ann Alexander* was killed five months later by Captain William Jernegon of the *Rebecca Simms*. "He seemed old, tired and diseased, what with ship timber splinters deeply imbedded in his head, and a number of the *Ann Alexander*'s irons still fast in his carcass."

The strangely human thread running through all these tales is the myth of the "rogue whale," or "biting whale," or "fighting whale." He is always a large bull, a solitary, surly, aggressive chap who cannot fit into any group. There was Payta Tom, and New Zealand Tom, Timor Jack, and Mocha Dick. The last was a great white beast whose adventures were followed for thirty-nine years, and who became the hero of *Moby-Dick*, the greatest sea story of all time.

95

The fighting whale, it is said, may meet the ship halfway, all unprovoked, or he may delay his rushing charge until he has been stabbed. He may ram the wooden hull time and again, even after his skull has been fractured. And when the ship is foundering he may continue to churn the surface, biting the floating debris and mechanically crushing the bodies of swimming men.

As a zoologist, I wonder at the motivation of the rogue. Into what pathological, what psychopathic, pigeonhole should I place him?

When a bitch dog with a fresh litter of puppies is approached by a stranger she attacks at once. When a *hungry* dog with a bone is approached in the same way he too attacks. These reactions are obvious; they have survival value to the race. But why does the rogue whale attack the ship?

Probably the answer lies in his strong territorial instinct, basically sexual. The sperm-whale bull is the only large whale that attacks ships. He is also the only one known to guard a harem and to battle with rival bulls for possession of females. When the "ship animal" invades his territory, it disrupts the dominance order; he rushes to attack.

Some zoologists stress the point that similar contests among land animals are for territory alone, rather than for females as individual prizes. The argument loses its punch in relation to animals on the fluid, three-dimensional sea. Where is the "territory" here?

Perhaps the rogue attacks the ship as a rival. Perhaps he is an individual in which the territorial imperative is acutely keen.

Another possibility, of course, is that the rogue is "deranged"—the cetacean counterpart of a man defective at birth or brain-damaged in later life. Or, as a final guess, he may be a "paranoid male" who feels himself hopelessly inadequate and "runs amok," or "goes into a windigo," or by whatever term escapes from reality like a man who kills his friend and brother and even tries to eat them in a blaze of white fury of which he later has no memory.

ᘛᘙᘚ

OUT where the sea birds wheel in endless circles, patient and watchful, held aloft by unseen strands, the mother of the Little Calf is dozing. She is resting head down at the surface after a rich, bursting feast of albacore, a kind of tuna. It is early morning.

Around midnight last, when darkness was deep and the black sea was dancing with the reflections of a million crystal stars, she saw the glow of something new on the horizon. She turned toward it. Soon she was in a dull fire of light shining from the water and reflecting from the low mist above. The air was quick with light.

She saw the first fish speeding in a school of thousands, each one breaking the dark of the sea in a phosphorescent streak. For a yard or more ahead the shock wave of each fish's body excited the bright particles of the sea, while behind, in the wake, the play of purple and green was an abstract painting of incredible beauty. Amid a wash of color, she set off in pursuit of the nearest fish . . . and then the next . . . and the next. She swam at top speed, throwing her forebody right or left, up or down, as she neared each victim. Most of the fish darted away to safety. At the instant when one loomed at the portal of her jaws, it would whip its silver-and-steel body like a saber and shoot off into the dark. In three hours of steady, exhilarating chase she seized and swallowed two dozen fish, the largest thirty pounds in weight.

The white flesh of the albacore is sweet, rich, and fat. The mother of the Little Calf was suddenly aware that her appetite had overshot her need. She was full and exhausted. So now she is resting while the sun rises slowly in the white mist.

Another cow in the harem is also resting nearby with a stomach full of albacore. Within her tired body she begins to feel a new sensation, something more than fatigue. It is a low-down thumping, not unpleasant, new but strangely old. A fetus in her womb is starting to make the first swimming motions in the amniotic fluid. During the previous night, while she pushed her great body in excitement to the limit of its power, a subtle message poured into her bloodstream and traveled to the placenta. It percolated through the barrier cells and entered the independent bloodstream of the new life.

The fetus has entered its ninth month of life. About the size of a full-grown man, it is still only halfway through its dark career. At this stage it would be recognizable as a female and is clearly a sperm whale in miniature, though it carries the lingering marks of other ancestors of related kinds. Its little body, once rosy-colored, is turning gray above and whitish underneath. The five fingertips can still be counted. Soon they will merge in the broad outline of the flipper. The ear spot is rimmed by a roundish hump—the fading vestige of a larger ear. The clitoris is sinking into a long groove, no more than a slit, which will later be flanked by nipples (thus · | ·). The eyes are nearly shut; the rubbery jaw twitches from time to time as the fetus swallows a salty fluid which passes through its loins and returns to the womb within an hour.

The baby teeth are all there in rows, but deeply buried, pulpy soft and pink. They are the only set the little whale will ever have. For seven years after she is weaned, until the white cylinders erupt at last from the gums, she will grasp her food with the help of toothless jaws and agile tongue alone.

One set of teeth, and these not fully formed until the whale is breeding. Why? For modern whales, the tooth arrangement satisfies the need. The jaws grow slowly, while the tooth buds keep pace in the deeper tissues. About the time the jaws are grown the teeth have reached their permanent stations. Such an arrangement is reasonable for a beast that lives to a large extent on soft-bodied prey and that swallows many of the prey animals in a gulp, entire. A land mammal, such as a dog, bites and tears its food even before it is fully weaned, and so it needs a set of teeth in early life. If these teeth were to remain in the growing jaw they would soon be standing far apart, useless for the task of chewing flesh. So they fall out in orderly fashion and the permanent teeth erupt in jaws that are then as large as they ever will be.

In the family of the Little Calf there is also an old female who is at the moment neither pregnant nor giving milk, a rare condition indeed for a full-grown female whale. Her last pregnancy was a tragedy, one that occurs once out of two hundred whale pregnancies. She carried twins. She carried them for fourteen months, then brought them forth prematurely and dead. Still, she could never have nursed them both to the age of independence.

ʃʃʃ

THE sperm whale is one-third head, you will recall, and to that fact there is a strange importance.

"This high and mighty God-like dignity inherent in the brow is so immensely amplified, that gazing on it . . . you feel the Deity and the dread powers more forcibly than in beholding any other object in living nature," wrote Melville from the deck of the *Pequod* as he took the full-front view of a severed head.

In memory, I stand again on a slippery whaling platform in Alaska watching a workman with a razor knife as long as his arm stab cleanly through the flesh of a sperm whale's head and let the spermaceti flow. Minute after minute and barrel after barrel it gushed clean and unpolluted, as clear as water, bubbling and trickling. Then a filmy haze formed on the surface; the oily liquid cooled; ropy strings emerged—icicles, frozen waterfalls. The cascades chilled and stopped in depressed white points—a noble statue of wax at rest. I turned slowly away, careful of my step on the slickest floor in the world, the sodden, greasy, wooden deck of a whaling plant all overgrown with filmy slime.

JANUARY

On some unrecorded day in the past this kind of whale was named by men who supposed that it carried its seed in its head. The name has stuck; as the "sperm" whale it is known. I smile at the ignorance of those men, but no one has yet unlocked the secret of that mighty dome with its content of oily, waxy, tendonous, and gristly stuff; its labyrinth of walls and valves and passages, some free and others blind; ten or fifteen tons of living flesh and blood. Of what supreme importance can it be, that nature should have bought it at a biological cost so high? What special part does it play in the life of the whale, that the beast can afford to carry the burden of its weight?

I asked the workmen on the whaling platform to continue butchering on the other end of the beast for ten minutes while I slashed through the mountain of the head to see what I could quickly find. I discovered that there is only one blowhole or nostril on the prow, slightly to the left. But just inside this port of entry is the right nostril—or what is left of it. It seemed to lead down as a breathing tube, and deeper down. As I followed its winding course through the drained and empty spermaceti case it suddenly came to an end on the bony upper jaw. The tube was ten feet long, and I would say that it is completely useless, though I am undoubtedly wrong. But why did nature, in building the sperm whale, dispense with half of the breathing parts? I started afresh at the blowhole and cut through the still warm meat, which steamed faintly in the arctic chill. I followed the *left* breathing tube for a good twelve feet before it plunged through the skull and disappeared.

"Hey, now!" the foreman called, and I reluctantly backed away from the gory head. The men trimmed off the meat and tore the head loose with a resounding "pop!"

Chains and tackle fell to the deck and now I could see the skull, rising higher than a man's head—a most peculiar skull. From the side it looked like a huge scoop shovel, or perhaps a sleigh. The long bony platform of the upper jaw was exposed, the bed where the tons of head-meat lay.

Some scientists have supposed that the spermaceti mass and all the complicated tissues weaving through it and around it are a kind of breathing reservoir, a "lung in the head" where oxygen is held and slowly paid out during long periods of submergence. Recently other scientists have listened to tape recordings of sperm whales undersea and have reported that the call notes are unlike those of other whales. Is the head perhaps an organ for the production of enormous sound, for the production of sonar signals in the ocean deeps? Are some of the queer structures I dissected in fact pipes and baffleboards, stops and mutes, resonating chambers? The answer lies in the future, though I think not far away.

Thomas Beale showed remarkable insight when he wrote: "All sperm whales both large and small, have some method of communicating by signals to each other, by which they become apprised of the approach of danger, and this they do, although the distance may be very considerable between them, sometimes amounting to four, five or even seven miles. The mode by which this is effected, remains a curious secret."

Is man about to break the code?

ऽ-ऽ-ऽ

EVERY whale everywhere moves in a sea of total sound. From the moment of its birth until its final hour, day and night, it hears the endless orchestra of life around its massive frame. Silence is an unknown thing. The snapping and crackling of tiny shrimps and crablike organisms, the grunting and grating, puffing and booming, of a hundred fishes, the eerie whining and squealing of dolphins, the sad voices of sea birds overhead, the chatter of its own companions, the undertone of moving water and the drone of wind, all these notes and many more come flooding through its senses all the time. It *feels* the music, too, for water presses firmly on its frame—a smooth continuous sounding board.

The Little Calf is slow to learn the meaning of the various sounds. In fact, he never learns them all, but only those that have to do with food and mother, danger, something near and something far, echoes from a floating log, the voices of his friends—the ordinary sounds. As a blind man living in the forest comes to know the birds by their songs, the Little Calf comes to recognize the whales that cross his path. Some vibrations are vaguely familiar from the first. These are the voices of the toothed whales, the ancient order of his kind. But the vibrations of the baleen whales are coarse and rasping, meaningless. Often in his baby life he hears a sort of barnyard chorus at a distance, weird and unfamiliar, unforgettable. It creaks and cries, barks, groans, and whoops. He never learns its source.

Today he hears another sound like an interstellar cry. It starts as an eerie moan without dimension, formless. It rises to a scream and then fades away, trembling, descending, echoing faintly, leaving the Little Calf frozen. From whence the cry? It never comes again. Perhaps a creature from the deeps as yet unknown to man? Perhaps an ordinary animal, far beyond its normal haunts? Perhaps a silent creature forced to break its silence by some agonizing pain?

ॐॐॐ

IT is hard for men to realize the importance of vibrations to the Little Calf. All whales are constantly sorting out the tingling messages, most of which are worthless and yet must be read.

Vibrations tell the Little Calf nearly all he needs to know. He has no sense of smell. Long before he was born, while he lay curled quiet in the womb, a pair of fleshy lobes began to swell at the front of his tiny brain. Olfactory lobes they should have been according to the mammalian plan, but other cells and tissues pushed them back. They disappeared. From the awesome depths of geologic time a faint command carried to the embryonic brain. The coding of the chromosomes tapped briefly, stuttered, stopped.

Indeed, what need has a whale for a sense of smell?

The vision of whales is on its way to obsolescence too. The Little Calf's eyes stare from padded slits above the corner of his jaw. He has never seen his own tail and never will. Each eyeball is covered with a tough transparent skin, anchored by heavy muscles, lubricated with greasy tears. When he pokes his head above water he is myopic and astigmatic. In water, though, he sees well enough to find his mother's belly and the milk supply. While his complicated sense of hearing and his phonation system are maturing he needs his eyes to reinforce the messages, to help at the start to identify the sources of sounds.

Probably he could make his way well enough if his sight was totally lost. Many times I have watched seals in the wild, completely blind and yet in good condition, fat and healthy. Vibrations of air and water serve for them in place of light.

In 1839 the zoologist and surgeon Thomas Beale wrote: "A whale perfectly blind, was taken . . . both eyes of which were completely disorganised, the orbits being occupied by fungous masses, protruding considerably, rendering it certain that the whale must have been deprived of vision for a long space of time . . . yet the animal was quite as fat, and produced as much oil, as any other captured of the same size."

So beautiful is the sea in January that my thoughts are drawn to the world ocean—the vast, encircling, enchanting fluid basin into which the dry lands and Mount Everest and the Dead Sea would all sink without a trace if all the earth were leveled.

What is the total amount of life in the total sea, I wonder —the plants and animals combined, the biomass? Is it far beyond the present hungry needs of man? Where do the sperm whales fit into the larger scene? Who takes their count; who numbers their dark heads?

To seek the answers is a game that many play. The ocean and its contents do not yield to easy measurement; the final data lie beyond our present grasp; an educated guess is now the best that men of science try to make.

They start, logically, I think, to measure oceanic life at its lowest trophic level; at the bottom of the ladder where simple atoms enter living plants. Carbon and nitrogen and phosphorus, the limiting factors—the fertilizing factors—of life are easily weighed. The seas are very old. They have circulated for so long that now the shades and tones of chemical admixture are a pattern fairly uniform and fairly well understood. We scoop a water sample from a hundred places here and there, multiply by a billion or so, and get an answer in terms of life, assuming of course the steady burning energy of the sun as a constant, making possible all life in whatever form on earth.

Says the Russian oceanographer V. G. Bogorov: The total plants in the ocean are a standing mass of 1.7 billion tons; the animals twenty times that.

But how can there be more animals than plants? How can a horse outweigh the grass it eats? The answer lies in the short life of the oceanic plant and the long life of the animal. In yield of new material, new living stuff each year, the plants outrace the animals ten to one. That is to say, the time dimension enters in. Life is not static. The ocean is a seething ferment with infinite levels of equilibrium between the particles men call "living" and those they call "dead." (The line is not easy to define.)

Says the American fishery scientist W. M. Chapman: The total harvest of fish from the ocean each year is sixty million tons, yet man could boost this thirtyfold if he could muster the full potential of his nets and lines and ships.

(Chapman and I were shipmates once. We drove the motor schooner *Black Douglas* from San Pedro to Seattle, all blacked out, a week after Pearl Harbor, in December 1941. The shore lights were out too. We steered by fathometer and by God.)

JANUARY

John D. Strickland of the Institute of Marine Resources of the University of California at La Jolla, however, is more conservative than Chapman. Tenfold, he says, not more.

At the other extreme, Wolf Vishniac of the University of Rochester, New York, and Lamont C. Cole of Cornell believe that we may be pushing hard to the limits of the seas. "Is the situation gloomy?" "Hell, no, it's hopeless."

Chapman raises a moral question also. The thoughtful scientist of today is not content to stay within his ivory tower; he *must* relate to man, communicate, involve himself to the limit of his ability with the large, open-ended problems, the final problems, of man adjusting to a world containing man. So Chapman says, in effect: Why do we try to raise the levels of global production of whales and fish and seaweeds and all the shining treasures of the sea? Whom do we aim to benefit? . . . First, we save the source itself. We do not overcrop. The capital stock comes first. And then we open the doors to all peoples of all nations everywhere to search for treasures in the sea. We place no barriers, political or national, provincial, racial, chauvinistic, in the way of cropping any underfished resource.

As a mental exercise I take Bogorov's estimate for the biomass of all the animals in the world ocean and lay it alongside the estimate for all sperm whales. Twenty-five thousand sperm whales are killed each year; the stock is being abused. The annual kill is perhaps one-tenth of the stock, which is then 250,000. Taking the average age as ten years and the average weight as ten tons, we have two and a half million tons of whales. Finally, compared to all animals in the ocean at a given time, the sperm whales represent one part in 13,600. This seems very high. I would not have thought that whales were so important, for they are spread so very thin. On the other hand, the weight of one whale is that of a trillion plankton animals.

The student of whale populations, the biostatistician, moves carefully through the jungle of figures in which he searches for his prey. He fears the pitfalls and the deviating paths. He searches always for the "random sample," the faithful mirror of the larger fact. It eludes his grasp. This is the nature of life information. He works forever with data from a stock that no longer exists, a ghost population that has moved in time and space since he last measured its parts.

He starts with one good solid fact: the number of sperm whales killed each year. He has also a few counts of whales seen from ships and aircraft; the numbers passing in migration near the shore and seen on breeding grounds. Through biologists he gets data from autopsies on the whaling deck—extremely useful. These tell him of the rate of body growth, the age when whales begin to breed, the pregnancy rate, the age at menopause, the incidence of disease, the death rate, and many of the other vital facts he needs to calculate the total stock and the wisest rate of use by man.

The percentage of marked whales recovered at the factory is useful too. Biologists of the whaling nations are shooting steel markers into the backs of whales at sea. The returning data, however, must be stretched so far that little confidence can be placed in them. The markers *do* indicate the wandering of whales and suggest the outlines of their home territories—the discreteness of the various stocks.

The biostatistician finally gives the whaling manager a choice. "Here," he says, "is the upper estimate of possible yield and here is the lower. Take your pick."

JANUARY

James Thurber makes a pertinent comment on the lower forms of life in the sea—the pelagic ooze:

"The penguin eats plankton, a nourishing if somewhat despondent food, charmingly described by the dictionary as 'the passively floating and weakly swimming animal and plant life of a body of water.' Man, being Man, doesn't care much for submissive victuals, but loves to beat the hell out of some of his main dishes, and has devised a dozen weapons with which to kill them, on sea or land or in the air, from the fish hook and the harpoon to the rifle and the shotgun. The penguin and the dolphin, beholding the dismaying spectacle of human beings at table, will surely exclaim, when they learn English, 'What foods these mortals eat!' "

FEBRUARY

WHILE sperm whales by the thousands and tens of thousands are feeding in the temperate waters of the North Pacific, a few hundred old bulls are plying back and forth in the near-freezing waters of the higher latitudes where the currents of the Bering Sea mingle with those of the Pacific. These older males, some of whom have traveled at times with the Little Calf's family, are a motley group of immigrants from many seas. Some were born among the scented breezes of the Caroline Islands, some among the Marshalls, and others among the Gilberts, though most were born in the wide, free ocean far from the boundaries of any sovereign state. Their feeding range in the north is vaguely defined. It stretches in a ragged arc two thousand miles across, from Kodiak on the east to the Commander Islands on the west, all of it lying south of the dangerous eddies that carry floating ice from the Pole.

The bulls rise and fall on the never-ending swells of the open sea. The winter days are short and gloomy now, interrupted by williwaws—violent gusts that spring from the empty valleys of the Aleutians and rip in screaming fury across the sea. The moving wind and the moving waves blend in a flowing sheet of smoke for an hour or so, and then the wind drops away as quickly as it came. Through sleet and snow, through great soft, rolling, dripping mountains of fog, through nights so black they define the word, the whales pursue their prey. They never pause. They do not need to rest; in fact, the steady play of their muscles warms their blood in the icy seas.

They wander through the wide passes of the Aleutians into the Bering Sea, but they stay clear of the narrow straits where the currents are treacherous, and where the tides from north and south meet in contests of strength that bulge the sea into frightful, hissing walls of green as high as the deck of a ship. Here the tide sucks away all at once in a change of direction that lays bare the ugly, ragged rocks which rarely see the light of day.

Now and then the clouds are torn apart by a clean wind,

and low in the north a moon rainbow stands quickly against the black sky. Its colors are all in proper order, but soft and uncertain, diluted by the blue reflections of the night.

The whales' passage to and fro may take them in sight of the islands of the Aleutian Chain, the cleanest and fairest of all islands. Volcanic by birth, their pure white cones rise above nine thousand feet, with slumbering inner fires, and puffs of smoke and flame, and cinder fields patterned among the eternal snows. They are sharp and clean, treeless and windswept, the home of foxes and birds.

The yellow-eyed fox picks his way daintily along the shores in winter, turning over stones to lick the sand fleas or to nose among the kelpy drifts for stranded fish and the carcasses of gulls. No fragment, however tattered, grimy, or stinking, repels the little fox in winter. His stomach is taut; anything resembling flesh is food. If he is lucky there will come to his island a great winter tide bearing the carcass of a whale. The fox and his companions will eat their way through the hull of the stranded beast and will revel and wallow for weeks in the oily putrescence. They will beat a well-worn track to and from it on the sand. Their silvery fur will become matted and dark with oil. They will be scarecrows until nature provides them with a new coat in autumn.

From a distance, the islands are all white, but closer they show patterns of brown and gray—beautiful patterns of rank grass and stark stalks of Heracleum and raw clean boulders and whipping stems of the plants that live in the cold, wet air of the northland.

FEBRUARY

The red-faced cormorants drop in heavy-bodied flight from the cliffs and settle to the sea, jerking their heads from side to side, puzzled at the world around them. The tiny precious, whiskered auklets drift through the mist and settle beside the whales. These birds number in the whole world only two thousand or so—a hundred pounds?—a little band, a fragment species. Tufted puffins—the comic sea parrots—ride out the sea storms of winter in the Aleutians. These world-ranging pelagic birds burrow in the ground in summer. They lay their eggs in secret tunnels. In winter they seek the rolling life of the sea.

Other birds in the world of the whales are ghostly creatures of the night: the fork-tailed petrels. The size of swallows, they flutter and twist in blackness above the sea. They dip, and dip again, for tiny, luminescent plankton life and rise, fluttering.

ഗഗഗ

FEW ships enter the waters around the Aleutians in winter for most of the islands are barren of human life. Soft, rounded mounds of earth on the estuaries of streams, and nearby kitchen middens filled with crumbling bones and spines and teeth of sea animals, give evidence that men once lived there with their women and children, but the Europeans came two centuries ago and drove them to death or exile. The story of their passing is brief and sordid. It is a bitter chronicle of man's inhumanity to man.

No full-blooded Aleut is now alive.

Ethnologists say that among the native Aleuts some practiced whaling by an ingenious method. They were the priests of a whaling cult. They would dip the points of arrows and harpoons in a dark brew made secretly from the roots of poisonous plants (Aconitum, Ranunculus, and Anemone). Then the village hunters in skin-covered boats would surround a whale and hurl as many points as possible into its back. They would wait for it to die from paralysis and drowning. Days later, if the currents were right, the body would wash ashore and set the stage for a week of feasting. But if the winds and currents were contrary, the body might drift east and south for many a hundred miles, and eventually lodge on a distant beach where its burden of odd shape and substance would frighten the natives there.

Far above the road of the Aleutian whales, through the blue-black sky, the jet planes pass in all hours of the day and night, following the Great Circle from Alaska to the Orient and back again. Those planes that pause en route and rise in whining flight from the way stations of Cold Bay or Adak (and other places hidden in the military fold) disturb the whales and make them dive in alarm.

The Aleutian arc is a young and restless part of the earth. The sea floor creaks and rumbles there. Seismic shocks are common, and every time the seismographic needles sway in Hokkaido and Anchorage and Seattle, the sperm whales feel the rhythm too; they pause to hear the thunder of the deep.

I was out there one summer and saw where the beacon at Scotch Cap used to shine. On a dark night in the previous April a great wave rose silently from a trench off Unimak. It climbed the cliffs and swept away the light and all the men, ninety-two feet above the sea.

FEBRUARY

In the lives of the creatures of the northern seas, danger and disaster are common. Strange accidents befall the whales and seals, the sea birds and the fishes, of the Aleutians. Carcasses and groups of carcasses with symptoms of scalding heat are found floating on the sea. Were they victims of a submarine explosion of steam and sulfurous gas—a geyser in the sea? The bodies of seals and birds are found strewn together on a beach, intact, with no clue at all to the cause of death. Were they victims of mass poisoning by the notorious red tide?

ᔥᔥᔥ

ON the fourth of February, three of the sperm-whale bulls are feeding on smelt-like silvery capelin, in Kronotsky Bay off Kamchatka. Though the fish are small, only six or eight inches long, they are sweet and tender, and their bright sides flash by the thousands in massive, slowly moving shoals.

Off to the westward in the overcast the whales see a pale suffusion that means the presence of floating ice. It reflects against the gray ceiling. By this and other signs they sense the western limit of their feeding range. They slowly turn about, toward America.

The quiet of the winter afternoon is punctuated by the soft sighs of a dozen porpoises, feeding on capelin too. They are right-whale dolphins, so called because, like right whales, they have no dorsal fin. These sleek black-and-white companions of the whales are moving slowly, surfeited with food.

The grizzled face of a bull fur seal breaks the surface. He grasps a capelin firmly in his teeth and shakes his head in a quick blur of motion to snap the living body of the fish into bits that he can swallow. (He has no paws to hold them.) Drops of spray scatter in a circle around his head. A gull swoops to snatch a silver tidbit here and there. Like the bull whales, the bull seal has chosen to winter in the north at the edge of drifting ice. His summer home is a rocky island off Sakhalin, in the Sea of Okhotsk. For days at a time now in winter he is alone, without communion with others of his kind.

In the sea beneath a dark cliff on the south side of Amukta Island an Alaska cod is grazing through a slimy forest of Alaria stalks. It moves at random among the brown plants at a depth of twenty fathoms. It seizes here and there a crab or a snail, a starfish or a sea urchin. Its three-foot, putty-colored body is all goggle eyes and mouth, and a trembling whisker hangs from its chin. Through the dim light the cod sees a moving figure outlined in silvery bubbles. The cod darts forward and clamps the thing in a set of needle-sharp teeth. The prey is a cormorant, a bird that dives deeply to feed on squids and small fishes (including the young of the cod). Back and forth the fish and the bird wrestle among the weeds, but the cod is in its own element and it swims away with the neck, head, and tapering bill of the bird in its throat.

That night the cod swims into the pass between the islands of Amukta and Yunaska. Around eleven o'clock, a sperm whale cruising through the pass swallows the cod without a pause. Now the life circle is nearly complete. The cod that ate the bird that ate the cod that ate the copepod that ate the diatom will soon enter the bloodstream of the whale; bones and scales and feathers will pass out with the feces, to be attacked by molds and bacteria and broken down into chemicals which will fertilize the growth of new diatoms.

As the sperm whales turn eastward they hear a faint throbbing *whap-whap-whap*, a sound remote from any they have heard before. By instinct they dive, for a thing strange is a thing dangerous. In a few minutes they feel the vibrations more and more compelling. One of them rises for a breath of air. His blowhole begins to gape like a black wet funnel when he hears a sharp *bang* and feels a thump in the middle of his back. The air and water are filled with a tremendous WHAP-WHAP-WHAP! The first shock gives way to a small, stinging pain. The whale blows like a locomotive running wild and dives without waiting to ventilate his lungs.

Thirty feet above, a helicopter is climbing swift and straight into the sky. It is fluorescent orange with its name in black letters—the Russian equivalent of *Star Third.* Long cylindrical pontoons stretch beneath it. Its whirling blades hurl a blast of air against the sea and build a circle of concentric ripples, mingled with the swirl of the departing whale. A bright face peers from a window. The face of a girl?

The *Star* is a "chopper" under contract to the big Soviet research station at Petropavlovsk, where problems of the sea and its fisheries are studied through the year. Last summer, Ludmila Grekova, a girl of twenty-two who is a member of the staff, conceived the idea that whales could be tagged for research more easily by approaching them in a helicopter than by chasing them in a ship. Her idea moved slowly at first in the turgid channels of administration until it reached the office of a young man who was impressed both with the idea and with the sparkle in the girl's gray eyes. An order went to the tool shop and another to the planning room.

So now on the fourth of February a 12-gauge shotgun, pointing down from a helicopter window, has fired a stainless-steel cylinder into the fat back of the whale. The chopper with its pilot and two passengers, one of them Ludmila, moves on in search of other experimental targets. Before the pilot warns that the point-of-no-return is only minutes away, they strike two other whales and a "possible." On the last attempt, the aircraft lurches as the trigger is pulled, and the projectile strikes the side of the whale at an angle. (The marker, if indeed it penetrated, is hidden in a smother of foam.)

The first bull hit is now fifty miles to the east, swimming at full speed on a straight course, trying to shake loose the burning object fastened in its back. Within a week, the entry wound will cease to drain, and in another week the pain will be gone. Next summer, the bull will be taken by the crew of a Japanese whaling boat and the bright marker will be found at the bottom of a cooker by a filthy workman shoveling out the gurry. The biologist on board will shrug his shoulders in annoyance and protest again to the captain: "Why can't the flensers keep their eyes open? Why can't they watch for these markers?" Though he has recovered a marker, to be sure, he doesn't know which whale in the day's catch it came from, though probably it was the big old bull that brought ninety barrels of oil and was surely fifty years of age.

The second bull hit by a marker will carry Tag no. 559 for four years and three months. He will be killed by a gunner of the *Zelenogradsk* en route to the Antarctic whaling grounds and he will be famous, briefly, as the first sperm whale known surely to have crossed the equator. His fate will overtake him north of Guadalcanal, four thousand miles from Kronotsky Bay. He will have traveled a thousand miles a year, though no man will ever know the shape of his track, and the times when he rested, and the times when he forged ahead.

As the helicopter nears the shore of Kamchatka toward sunset, Ludmila scribbles quick notes in her record book, setting down the important events of the afternoon while they're still fresh in mind.

Her companion biologist, Yuri Sokolov, has taken a keen interest in the chase of the whales but he hasn't been able to try *his* device, a gadget which he hopes will help to describe the devious track of a moving whale. (Nothing like it has worked before.) It is a device of wires, batteries embedded in wax, a projectile point.

As the chopper enters Kronotsky Bay, Yuri sees a target: a group of little piked whales, the small baleen whales that frequent the sheltered waters of the coast. He motions to the pilot, telling him by hand signals to carry out the plan they agreed on before they left the base. The chopper dips her nose and points her white pontoons toward the target. Yuri loosens his seat belt with a quick tremor of fear and kneels at the open window, harpoon-gun in his lap. The airstream tears the goggles from his face and draws the tears from his eyes. He is dead on target; he pulls the trigger. *Vr-oom!* A heavy charge of black powder, slow-burning but packed with energy, hurls a two-pound projectile into the rump of the whale, slightly abaft the dorsal fin. The missile travels too fast for his eye to follow it. It is a neat, shiny cylinder packed with printed circuits, transistors, miniaturized organs that, according to plan, will function perfectly. The pole antenna snaps out on schedule and trails behind as the whale doubles its rippling body in naked fright and sounds to the depths where it has always found escape from danger.

Yuri turns to a receiver strapped on the floor of the aircraft and puts on earphones. He listens intently for the mechanical purr which the device has given on command in the sheltered laboratory where it was conceived. He listens . . . Whale and ocean are still; no whisper from the faultless cylinder so carefully designed by man returns his scientific love.

〰〰〰

Animals are molded by natural forces they do not comprehend. To their minds there is no past and no future. There is only the everlasting present of a single generation—its trails in the forest, its hidden pathways of the air and in the sea.

LOREN EISELEY

FEBRUARY

' How does the sperm whale find its way at sea? How does it plot its course? By what transparent threads is it drawn back, season upon season, to the mating grounds? What landmarks and seamarks illuminate its tracks?

I ask these questions but I do not give the answers. No man gives the answers. The biologists of the future will tell us where the sperm whale gets its clues. They will test theories, evaluate results, number probabilities that this force or that one is responsible for turning the whale's direction of movement.

The future biologist will look at the magnetism of the earth (the north-and-southness), the Coriolus Force (the mechanical effect of rotation), the azimuth of the sun at the season and its polarized light, the taste and temperature of the water, the flow of the prevailing winds, the contours of the sea floor, the position of the celestial bodies. He will ask: What do all these marine and terrestrial and extra-terrestrial signs mean to whales? These faint messages from the water world around, and the sky, and the outer space beyond; what do they say? What is the importance of each in guiding the sperm whale to its accustomed place?

Possibly the migration of the whale is a simple, uncomplicated, follow-the-leader sort of thing. Young whales trail the older ones. They learn the ancient paths by observation and feel.

Early in the present century a great zoologist began to wonder about the movements of whales. Eventually he learned a great deal about the places where they live though little about the clues that guide them to these places. He was Charles Haskins Townsend, director for thirty-five years of the New York Aquarium. On a visit to the public library in

New Bedford, Massachusetts, he found, to his delight, hundreds of logbooks from Yankee whaling ships of bygone years. In the daily journals of life at sea the captains had dutifully entered the date, the bearings, and the species of whales killed.

Townsend realized that by plotting on charts the positions where large numbers of whales had been taken, much could be learned of their distribution and something of their migrations. So he drafted beautiful charts of the world ocean, showing by colored dots the month and the location of whale ships on days when whales were killed. In his labor of love he sifted the records of one hundred and sixty years of whaling, and the capture of more than thirty thousand whales.

ᔕᔕᔕ

ON the tenth of February a fishing boat called the *Halcón* is cruising in the subtropical Pacific, along the coast of Mexico, at the southern limit of the range of the Little Calf's family. She is on a trial voyage, a strange voyage, testing whether a purse seiner can be adapted for catching whales. She is registered in a Central American state which is not a member of the International Whaling Commission and whose citizens are not bound by any laws respecting the capture of whales.

Before the voyage the owners of the *Halcón* had a discussion.

"Here we have a fine boat in use for only eight months of the year, when the sardinas are here. Why can't we run her also in the spring, as a whale-catcher? We see the big fellows out there where we spread our nets."

"But whales are frightened by the sound of a diesel. They are hunted only by steamers or sailing boats or pulling boats."

"Is that true, amigo? How does one know?"

The discussion was led by a Portuguese called Beppo, who had worked with a California shore-whaling company. His dark eyes glistened as he described the excitement of the chase and the mountains of red meat brought to the dock to be sold for dog food to make the owners rich.

So at the end of the fishing season the *Halcón* is fitted out with a new set of tackle. There is much scratching of heads: Who knows how to shoot a whale? How big a line we need to hold him?

Finally a cannon is mounted on the peak and a Norwegian named Axel Swanson is hired to shoot it.

The owners find Swanson in a waterfront cafe. He is known to all the fishermen as an ex-whaler from the Southern Ocean, and as a teller of tales to whom one listens politely, and for whom one buys a drink now and then for the sheer poetry of his words. So long in the Antarctic he endured the bitter winds and frozen spray that he now chooses to bask in the tropical sun until he dies. Axel has seen better days. He swears that he owns the best eyes for whales in the whole world, and it is no secret that he keeps them sharp by drinking a great can of seawater each morning as he staggers from his bunk. He dips it from the local pier, and it contains other things than seawater, foreign bits that may in truth keep him healthy by preserving his immunity against everything that creeps and crawls. But along toward noon when the sharp eyes of the great hunter are twitching in the white sunlight, the purifying effects of the oceanic brew have drained away and the grip of *vino tinto* is supreme.

As she leaves on her maiden voyage for whales the *Halcón* is showered with laughter and cheers from the dock, with words rude but basically encouraging. She turns west by south. Where will the first target be sighted?

Three hours and thirty miles later, Pedro, in the crow's nest, sees the sperm whales. They are undisturbed for they have never been chased in these waters. Pedro begins to shout and point: "Ballena-ballena-ballena!"—all one word. He jumps up and down in the barrel without thought for safety.

Axel drops the rope he is splicing and runs to the peak. He rips the canvas cover from the gun, throws off the safety catch, drops the sun-glare goggles from his graying forelock, and swivels the barrel back and forth in a testing motion on its well-oiled track. Though his eyes are bleary his mind is clear. He is again a man of action. He is again the number one gunner among all the gunners of the southern ice. The captain steps outside the wheelhouse to the controls on the bridge where he can follow the directions of Pedro, silhouetted against the sky. Pedro wears a black stocking cap with a red tassel which flies up and down as he jumps. With his red cheeks framed in black beard he is straight from Mother Goose. Twenty minutes later the ship is overtaking the whales and now Axel himself can see the white mushrooms of vapor—three of them, or maybe four.

He shouts to the skipper that he wants to give the sailing orders now, but Spanish has left him suddenly and his words are pure waterfront Norwegian. Fortunately the skipper can see the trailing wakes of the whales. With a fisherman's quick understanding of life in the sea he soon is predicting where the next whale will rise to blow.

Choo-oof! A frightened whale lifts in a majestic black arc only sixty feet ahead of the ship and the gunner turns his cannon to the spot. He struggles to lower the sight to the back of the whale but the goddam thing won't lower. The barrel strikes the teakwood rail. The men had never thought, when they mounted the gun, that it would be aimed at a target so near and so low. The whale sounds. Axel rips off a pattern of oaths and sucks at torn fingernails and drops to a hatch cover, shaking uncontrollably. The whale escapes.

Since the afternoon is calm and the sea is flat, the *Halcón* heaves to, twenty miles offshore. She rolls gently on the groundswell while two of her men attack the forward rail with chisels and saws. They clear a wide arc so the gun can be lowered another ten degrees. The February dusk falls quickly. They finish the job by yellow lamplight.

From the dark coastline a soft night breeze springs out and carries the fragrance of mahogany to the men of the *Halcón.* They crowd the galley for coffee and chunks of bread and fried prawns. Beppo is vindicated; he smiles broadly. A whale *can* in fact be run down by a noisy diesel ship. Tomorrow we will go after them again. This is more fun than we thought. But *Jesús*, they're big fellows! Will the tackle we got hold them?

A drowsy watchman is left on deck, for the ship might drift ashore if the wind were to change in the night. He watches with affection as a dozen petrels land on the rigging near the riding light. He knows them from childhood; they are called the *aves de San Pedro* because they walk on the sea. They sway on the ropes. Some are distressed by the new motion and disgorge the salmon-colored, oily contents of their throats, complaining softly all the while.

Axel has slipped off his boots. He lies on his bunk, nearly hidden in a blue cloud of tobacco smoke. He badly wants a drink but he knows there is nothing aboard, and in fact there is never any liquor aboard a fishing vessel worthy of the name.

Sharply after dawn the *Halcón* resumes her search for whales. On and on she drives over a fresh green sea. The call for breakfast comes: papayas, tortillas, fried fish, and black coffee. At eight o'clock the welcome shout again comes from the masthead: "Ballena!" Again Axel throws off his gloves, and spits, and fingers the trigger with fanatic eye. His legs are braced widely on the deck. No more than minutes ahead, the great dome of the whale shines before the ship's prow and the life of Axel is resurrected in a teeth-jarring BAM! An acrid cloud of smoke drifts to the bridge. A heavy line lies in the air like a magic wand.

The second explosion is deep and awful. The bomb in the head of the harpoon bursts in the back of the whale. Axel turns toward the bridge and raises two fingers, the sign of victory. He is at the peak of life, the very summit indeed. Any event and any thought beyond will be measured in terms of this moment.

Mercifully, the bomb explodes deep in the muscles a yard above the throbbing heart. At once, the breath of the whale is a pinkish froth and in five minutes her head lowers in the swell. The *Halcón* moves alongside and a man wearing faded pants and rope sandals leaps to the slippery back of the victim, holding a hose. It is an air hose with a sharp steel nozzle which he jabs deep into her flesh. At a signal, the skipper turns a valve and the whale's black body begins to bloat and rise in the water. When she rolls belly up the hose is withdrawn and the inflated shape is tied to the ship and towed toward land, fifty miles away.

Now the *Halcón* is slowed to four knots by her burden. The clock strikes midnight as she rounds the breakwater and enters the small harbor where she will dispose of her catch. She heads for the rendering plant. Here in the fishing season many thousands of tons of sardines and anchovies are cooked in great pressure pots. The hot stew is squeezed through a corkscrew vise. Yellow oil runs out in one direction and out the other rich, redolent brown meal tumbles onto an endless belt running to the sacking room.

When the run of fish is over, the plant shuts down, all but one cooker and one extractor. Here a few of the workers are kept busy processing sharks, rays, and other rough fish, and an odd porpoise now and then.

The manager is waiting on the dock to see the whale. (A

hundred men and boys and forty dogs are also waiting to see the whale.) The manager wouldn't bet five centavos on the *Halcón*'s chances, but here she comes proudly round the bend with the dark body lashed to her side and all her deck lights burning. She ties up to the dock to wait for daylight.

In the cool of morning the workmen loop a chain around the tail of the beast and winch her up a slippery platform that leads from the water to the butchering deck. When they pierce her belly with a long knife, such a rush of rank, sulfurous gas bursts forth that the white paintwork on the near side of the *Halcón* is colored a pale smoky brown and her men must scrub it off next day. The flesh of the whale is smoking hot, though she has lain for a day in the cool sea. A workman loops a steel cable around the jaw between her teeth and signals with his glove: *Arriba*. The jaw moves slowly out in agonizing creak and popping flesh. When the strain is final, the cable stops and a man leaps to the slippery head and dislocates the skull.

The rest of the story of blood and lymph would interest only a butcher, except for one fact. When the belly of the whale is slit open and a man puts a hook on the guts to free them from the carcass, the manager is astounded at their massive size. He is a man of curiosity, one of those rare species who will always be learning to his last breath, a man of inborn wonder. So he tells a workman to stretch the guts along the dock and wind them back and forth between two upright poles and measure the total length. The man shrugs—*Porque no?*—and unwinds the long pink tube. He frees it from the filmy mem-

brane with his sharp knife and starts to walk away with the upper end. His amazement grows as he pulls at the endless coil.
When the last bit is free—that end which is the size of a stovepipe—the total length is twelve hundred feet. He reports to
the manager, who can't believe it, and figures it out for himself. It's true! In later years the manager reads a book on
whales, but he never learns why the sperm whale has a quarter-
mile of guts, for no book has the answer.

The American commercial attaché in the nearest city
hears about the whale and visits the reduction plant with an
odd request. If more whales are captured, would it be possible
to freeze the meat for sale to his government? In the state of
Florida the department of agriculture is raising screwworms
on whale meat. Screwworms, the larvae of a kind of fly, are a
serious pest in the southeast, for they burrow into the flesh of
cattle, and they can kill a full-grown steer in less than ten days.
When the flies are newly hatched, they are sterilized with
gamma radiation and the impotent insects dumped from airplanes over the infested states. The sterile flies mate with wild
ones, and eggs are laid, but they never hatch. Slowly the wild
population is being thinned out, and soon the native flies will
find no mates at all. The scourge will be gone. In the meanwhile, the program calls for many millions of dollars and many
tons of whale meat.

The manager of the plant is amused. He calls the foreman.
The two men break into a rapid discussion. Finally the manager turns to the attaché. We are sorry, he says, but the supply

of whales here is not reliable. And the climate is so warm that the meat may spoil and the little flies will not like to eat it. And though the freezer plant is working fine today it may be broken down tomorrow. The attaché understands; he thanks them and goes away.

MARCH

WITHIN the herd of several hundred whales that includes the Little Calf and his mother a restless spirit is beginning to brush the body of this one and that. Indeed the tempo and behavior of the whole herd is beginning to change. This is more than a response to the gusty, brawling winds of March. It is a deep, biological pricking that swells the testes of the males and rouses the ovaries of the females and causes both males and females to move in patterns unaccustomed for a year. In May the testes of the bulls will ripen to a weight of sixty pounds or more—seven gallons in size. Already these organs are beginning to fatten, and the sperm cells within are multiplying and maturing. In the ovaries of the females the follicles are quickening and here and there a germ center is building the shape and structure of an egg.

As in all animals on earth, the body of the whale contains a biological clock, and when the alarm sounds the body tissues respond in predictable ways and the body motions follow suit. The unseen force now sounding the alarm for the family of the Little Calf is the growing length of day. As the broad white daylight impinges on the eye of the whale it excites a gland no bigger than a crab apple in the brain, the gland secretes a chemical messenger to the blood, and the messenger flows to the sex organs and to all the other tissues of the body. The grand, complex, ritual procession of the breeding season begins to move. The insurance of the species begins to pay.

(Among the Stone Age Eskimo that Vilhjalmur Stefansson and Peter Freuchen knew, the return of the spring sun after four months of night was the signal for a resurgence of sex. Any parallel with whales is superficial, though; "exuberance" —known to men—does not apply to whales.)

The herd now sorts itself into groups or camps. The adolescent males of ten years or so, and the older males, too, pull away from the herd, swimming faster, moving northward at a greater pace. The younger males are in the lead; the older ones are delayed by battling. The Little Calf grows used to the underwater sounds of challenge and the thump of bodies and the gurgle of air expelled from the lungs of struggling males. Most of the battles are contests of pure bluff, sham affairs in which no blood is shed and no bones are broken.

The females, too, sense the changes in March: the increase in volume and pitch of the submarine talk and the swirl of dark bodies. Some of them feel a rising tension in their own frames. They move northward toward the waters off southern California. In some mysterious way each female knows her own time.

The Little Calf has often sported with another calf of his own age, a little female. Lately he is puzzled by her strange behavior. What is wrong? She engages in play but after a moment she turns to the mother of the Little Calf and pushes angrily at her breast. She gets a few swallows of milk and then the mother pulls away and slaps the alien baby with her flipper.

The thin, sad baby lost her own mother in an accident at sea three weeks ago and is now dying of dehydration, though she is immersed in the sea. Some basic sense of rightness removed from what we humans call compassion warns the Little Calf's mother that the species is more important than the individual. She knows her own calf; she nurses it for the allotted time; she will not nurse a calf with foreign voice and feel. This is the law. The orphan is doomed.

AT the Washington conference for the study of cetaceans, one session was devoted to the conservation of whales. The delegates were asking, in effect: Why should we try to understand the lives of whales—their obscure patterns of behavior, their grotesque, encapsulated bodies—if they will soon be gone? Why should we sweat over a group of animals doomed to disappear in the crush of progress? Why should we shed a tear for living things that do not fit into our engineered world? Man alone is important, and when whales and seals, and tiny birds whose whole world population can be held in a man's arms, are destroyed, who will care?

Noel Simon of the International Union for Conservation of Nature opened the discussion. "In recent years there has been increasing awareness of the need for wildlife and wild places. Man's preoccupation with problems of his own survival may have made him slightly more sympathetic toward the other animals with which he shares this planet. There is also perhaps a dawning realization that, while it is permissible to use the income derived from some of the things of interest, beauty, and value which are part of man's natural heritage, the capital must be handed down intact to future generations."

M. N. Tarasevich, the Russian biologist, called attention to bald facts of the sperm-whale industry: "Due to the decline . . . of the stock, the northern region ceases to be of importance to the whaling industry."

(Why does the Soviet Union, a leader in modern whaling, continue to abuse the resource while her own biologists warn that disaster is near? Of all nations, she in principle should be among the first to control exploitive greed. Where men of government and those of industry draw the same breath surely it should be possible to enforce a conservation need. Yet it is not enforced and the whales are dying. I conclude that Russians are like other people, including Americans. In their fishery councils they say, "When the others agree to stop the killing, we will go along, but meanwhile . . .")

John Walsh of *Science* magazine stated: "So grim are the statistics of the industry that only three nations—Japan, Norway, and the Soviet Union—still engage in pelagic whaling. In the case of the largest whale of all, the great blue whale, some observers feel it may be too late now for that leviathan no matter what is done." That is to say, when a stock of whales has declined to a certain level—a certain threshold—the number of males and females able to find mates is then so low that the birth rate is below the death rate, and the species is doomed. "Conservation principles and long-run economic interests both dictate that lower kill quotas be set to raise sustainable yields in the long run. But logic and sentiment seem to need the support of workable law."

According to the Dutch anatomist E. J. Slijper, a century ago Svend Foyn went to sea on the maiden voyage of the whaleship *Spes et Fides* (Hope and Confidence). He carried a new weapon—a terrible weapon—a harpoon with a bomb in its head. It was very efficient. It was too efficient. Now the whole picture is a very sad one and we may say that only the "Hope" of Svend Foyn remains.

Mack Laing of the United Nations declared: "It is clear that many nations must act with a common conscience if we are to save one of earth's great animal resources from extinction and to preserve an industry so rich in the history of human endeavor."

I turned my eyes from the conference program toward a picture on the wall. It was a woodcut made when Shakespeare was alive. It depicts a stranded sperm whale, high and dry on a foreign beach with an English castle in the distance.

In primitive art, the odd and great events were those preserved—the strange and unexplained, the miraculous and fearful. I can see, in mind's eye, the town artist, called to the seashore in 1612 to sketch the beast that came last night to the beach on a flood tide and was resting there with dimming eye.

One man, with his wife beside him, is pointing with a stick. Approaching the whale are other men with knives and tubs, all aglow with their luck in being here when God saw fit to deliver up a wealth of oil and ivory. Dashing among them are small dogs, four legs in the air at a time, frantic with the fragrance of blood and oil and manure.

Three and a half centuries later, in the European lowlands, a tragic sperm whale was blown from the North Sea across a dike to die unseen on a polder. Then came a boy, and a man, and other men, and at last a scholar from a museum. The whale was hung from wires above a dock; he swung heavily with frozen death-grin, his six-foot penis, oddly curved and sickly gray, dangling low in last display. The circling crowd could not believe his size. They talked in quiet voices in the presence of a thing beyond their grasp.

Cables groaned and winches shuddered and vapor spurted from iron valves as the creature slowly fell to the dock. *Fifty-seven tons.* "Stand back! He'll maybe roll!" The broad black tail was last to slap on the dock. The crowd exhaled, priding itself on a job well done.

𝄞𝄞𝄞

TODAY the shifting winds and the sea currents and the flowing streams of life-providing food of the sea have worked together to bring the family of the Little Calf to a point two miles west of Isla de Guadalupe, which is a barren scabland one hundred and fifty miles at sea off Baja California, which is a bleak but hauntingly beautiful part of Mexico.

I find myself again, as in a dream, on that tiny island where I landed once to look at the last of the Guadalupe fur seals. Here on a hot, dry slope, a landscape from hell, I stare at circles and squares of piled-up rocks, the walls of huts erected in the 1800s by whalers. The roofs I suppose would have been sailcloth, stretched tightly above the walls, with a space to vent the suffocating air. Scratched on the gray volcanic rocks I read the names of ships and men, clear names in the beautiful curving script of their time. The oldest I find is *"Ship Essex . . . Henry Waldbon . . . Bristol R I . . . 1835."*

I stand in the shimmering heat, removed in time a century and more. The ghostly figures of bearded men in rough, sour clothes pass before my eyes. They speak directly of their captain: "Where does the sonofabitch think we're gonna sleep?" The pattern of seafaring men does not change.

Aside from its history—and of course its seals—the island is a lost place. Created in eons past by volcanic fire, with jagged red-and-black beds of rocks and leering gargoyles of lava, it rises four thousand feet above the sea. The north, and highest, point is often hidden in a cloud, and from this misty source a trickle of water finds its way to the ocean in certain months of the year.

The land animals are wild goats, cats, and mice—nothing more. All were dumped here by man and all have reverted to a wild and desperate state, and all are struggling to live on this rugged, almost treeless rock. Driven by hunger, a goat inched its way along a crumbling ledge toward the last spear of green, suddenly to fall to its death. I see its bones, and bones by the hundreds, where the sea currents have washed them ashore in quiet coves. I photograph the pattern of white skeletons curled there, for I like the design. I put aside for a moment the thought of man's stupidity in bringing the beasts to the island in the first place.

The pathetic mummy of a house mouse is impaled on a cactus spine where the little beast tried to reach a succulent bit of green within. (I remember some words by Peter Crowcroft, director of the Brookfield Zoo in Chicago: "There is something terribly familiar about the awful situation of a mouse in the world.") Bleached, white, feather-filled droppings of cats are scattered around the mouths of tunnels where petrels are still trying to nest.

Were it not for the seals and the trickle of fresh water, I

am sure that hot, dry, stinking Guadalupe would never have lured the *Essex* to drop anchor off its shores.

Toward evening, off Guadalupe, the Little Calf is surrounded by a chorus of dolphin music of extraordinary richness and volume. It swells from, and through, and above a chance aggregation of seven species of dolphins, some of them in schools of hundreds. The larger schools are breeding groups; the smaller schools are only passing through. Within a radius of a mile two thousand black-and-white bodies crisscross the upper layer of the sea, where a vast cloud of pink plankton has risen as dusk falls, and where fish in turn have gathered to feed upon the plankton life. It is a mild evening, for March. The ocean is alive with splashing forms.

In the frenzy of sexual and social excitement some of the dolphins find partners of other (though closely related) species, and next year there will be born little hybrids that will puzzle a Japanese biologist when he finds the carcasses of odd pattern in his net.

The Little Calf can scarcely hear the sound of his own family in the din of the dolphins underwater as they locate food and talk to each other, coming and going at high speed. The Little Calf knows all the sounds, though he has never heard so many at once. The crack of a shot, followed by the rattle of an explosion, shakes his inner ear and reverberates from the ceiling of plankton.

Motorcyclists roar in along the beach from the east and

disappear toward the west. Through a powerful background murmur there burst sad howlings, shriekings, and lowing sounds like cattle in distress.

The sperm whales continue on their course and by midnight have left the center of sound behind. They are in quieter surroundings. En route they pick up a few of the pilchards, anchovies, and lantern fish upon which the dolphins are also feeding, though these small fishes hold only passing interest for the great whales.

Toward dawn on the last day of March the wet sea fog begins to lift. The world becomes three parts: black beneath, gray above, and white between. Dainty sandpipers rise and fall on the ocean swell and peep softly as the tone of illumination changes.

One of the sperm whales sees a ruddy glow on the horizon, though indeed not in the east where the sun should be rising. With food in mind, he swims toward it for a mile until he catches a vagrant breeze and finds himself at the edge of a foul streamer of smoke pouring from the center of the glow. He snorts in fright and turns away.

The refrigerator ship *Shoku Maru* is wallowing in a fourteen-foot swell. She is alone and all aflame; a fire in her hold is out of control. Her crew left yesterday in life rafts, with a Buddhist prayer. Now they drift toward the west, waiting for the American Coast Guard to pick them up. They open wood-veneer boxes of salt fish and dried seaweed and rice. They hope to be saved, for before the captain ordered "abandon ship" the radioman told the world in broken English of their plight. The message spread over the globe in a tenth of a second. It was heard in silence by a yeoman at Byrd Station, near Little America, and by seafaring men on a dozen seas. It was heard by ship brokers in Tokyo, and the stock of Matsushita broke half a point.

Kasuo Fujima opens a roll of cloth in his kit and removes a length of cod line with triple hooks. He baits the hooks with salt fish and drops them over the edge of the raft. The baits rise and fall two hundred feet below. They move there for an hour and wash clean and white. Fujima-san pulls in the line. No one says a word. When a great ship is passing from the world it is like the passing of a sweetheart. One pauses, and tries desperately to store an image of beauty in a recess of the mind where it can be recovered.

Now and then a gray, sloppy sea slaps at the hull of the rolling *Shoku* and leaps beyond, to the fiery core of her distress, and the water bursts into a tower of red. A muffled explosion throws a rocket of white lines high into the fading night. In another hour a metal seam will buckle with a popping of rivets and the ship will die in a hell of sound and light, and her black form will slide mercifully down to the floor of the sea.

APRIL

THE family of the Little Calf is now feeding near latitude Thirty North, northwest of Isla de Guadalupe and south of the Channel Islands of California. Young and old have come nine hundred miles on a meandering course since they left the scene of the battle of the bulls in early January. They have joined a herd so large that from a ship the white streams of vapor seem to cover the whole western ocean and continue beyond the horizon.

In the north the sky is darkening. Late in the afternoon a bull marked by a white spot about the size of a dinner plate on the middle of his back—a mass of scar tissue from an old wound—swims for a minute beside another bull, then turns away and follows a cow. Hour after hour the pair swim side by side, keeping touch by flippers and flukes, or simply rubbing sides. They are silent. Neither feeds; neither dives, though they run submerged for minutes at a time. Presently the male moves to a position above the female, gently stroking her back. He withdraws and chases her for five minutes. (There is no question about who is the aggressor.) He speeds up and rubs his belly against hers in a burst of motion. Now he races ahead and rolls, exposing first his belly and then his back. He shoots through the water with his flippers held stiffly at right angles to his sides. He is simply throwing his body into odd shapes to attract the female. The tempo of courtship rises. The cow turns responsively upside down and the bull swims across her inflamed belly. They return to normal swimming positions and the bull locks his jaw in hers. They nuzzle, clap jaws, slam their heads together. The love play continues for half an hour.

The black cloud from the north is drawing close and the edge of the sea is hidden in a veil of rain.

At last the pair rise high from the sea, black snouts against black sky, belly to belly, flippers touching, water draining from the warm, clean flanks. They copulate in seconds, then fall heavily into the sea with a resounding splash.

The herd is moving north or northwest at an average speed of three knots, about as fast as a man could walk. In a few days a pattern begins to take shape in the movements of each individual whale. The blowhole flares and closes; the eye seems to wink; the sudden flash of long furrows in the skin suggests the play of muscles underneath. The Little Calf is nursing; his mother warily keeps her distance from the rest of the group.

In the midst of the wind and the rain another pair of whales also mates, this time in the horizontal position.

Then the sea is blotted out by the storm.

ᔕᔕᔕ

The moot point is, whether Leviathan can long endure so wide a chase, and so remorseless a havoc; whether he must not at last be exterminated from the waters, and the last whale, like the last man, smoke his last pipe, and then himself evaporate in the final puff.

HERMAN MELVILLE

The history of whaling is long and complex. It is inseparable from the difficult question of property rights, or who owns the whales and what do we mean by "freedom of the seas"? It deals with an industry worth $150 million a year.

Whaling began among savage people using primitive weapons and it will perhaps end in our own time with whalers using machinery and instruments so monstrous and so elaborate that only specialists will understand them. The earliest men pursued whales with spear points of stone or ivory. To the spears they tied floats of wood or inflated skin. When, after days of struggle, the whale tired of pulling the floats, the hunters approached and gave the *coup de grâce*. Somewhere, and some time, a hunter did not clean his spear after a chase and thus he learned by accident that a bit of rotten meat left on the point is a charm which brings death more quickly to the next victim. Today we know about blood poisoning, or septicemia. The hunter who hit upon the magic of the rotten corpse and its inoculum did not. He became the first priest of a whaling cult.

Individuals of the northern tribes probably learned to kill whales with drugs extracted from poisonous plants by first learning to kill small fish in tidepools. The origin of aconite poisoning is hidden in the mists of time.

The Japanese, historically among the leaders in exploiting the riches of the sea, made ingenious nets so strong that they could hold large whales.

It is not difficult to imagine what our savage ancestors *did* with the body of a whale, whether fresh or stale. They ate the meat; they ran the oil into baskets and pots and burned it for light and heat; they worked the bones into tools and utensils and drew the sinews into threads.

With each invention of a better kind of boat and a better kind of spear, the pursuit of whales was carried farther from shore. When at last in the 1860s Svend Foyn perfected the harpoon with a bomb in its head, he opened the last century of whaling. He patented his bomb on Christmas Eve and wrote in his diary. "I thank Thee, O Lord. Thou alone hast done all."

I hope that no statue has been erected to Foyn, and yet I

can sympathize with the people who in good faith honored the man who brought fortune to Norway, though disaster to the whale.

In America the first sperm whale was captured in 1712 when New Englanders, whaling for the coastal right whale, were blown out to sea in a storm. The Yankee whale fleet reached its peak in 1846, when there were 735 sloops, schooners, brigs, barks, and other whaling ships at sea. Once a proud whaling nation, the United States now has a single shore station, in California.

In the early 1800s the richest products of the whale were oil and baleen. When the first petroleum well spouted in Pennsylvania in 1859 it spelled the doom of whale oil as an illuminating fuel. The baleen that brought five thousand dollars a ton in 1897 for corset stays was replaced by plastics. Today, however, the bones and guts and juices are converted to a hundred uses; the Japanese now eat more than one hundred thousand tons of whale meat a year.

In 1904 Christian Larsen built a whaling station at South Georgia and opened the great Antarctic whaling industry which up to now has brought the death of more than a million whales. Whaling was cut loose from the land in 1923 and the major industry is now carried on from factory ships that roam freely for months on end through international waters of the world. Day and night through the hunting season a small fleet of catcher boats supplies each factory ship with whales. At last report, there were two hundred and fifty-one boats in operation.

In man's attempts to catch more whales more cheaply, he has tried to poison them with strychnine and cyanide and curare. He has tried to electrocute them. Spotters in airplanes and helicopters now search them out and report the position of the herds to whaling vessels below. The ships hunt them down by ASDIC, the system that can feel the whales in total darkness. A "whale-scaring machine" frightens the beasts into flight with ultrasound and tires them so the hunter can overtake them. What will be next? Will the orbiting satellite speak through space to tell the hunter where to find the last whale? Will the hunter cut a phonograph record of the mating call of the whale, or the cry of the calf for its mother, and play back the sounds beneath the bow of his ship?

Don't misunderstand me—I applaud all inventions which promise to kill more cheaply, more cleanly, and more humanely. But if we will not accept responsibility for the wise use of the new weapons we will be cursed by future generations as the people who destroyed the greatest creatures that ever lived.

Only twenty-seven years after the discovery of Alaska the last sea cow was clubbed to death by a hunter in the shallows of the Bering Sea. It weighed perhaps four or five tons and it was the only mammal outside of the tropics that lived on seaweed. We shall never know the secrets of its life: how it survived the freezing winters, how it dealt with the hazard of salty food, what defenses it raised against its enemies, and all the other factors of its body structure and habits. Men will never get insight into the processes of their own lives through study of those of the sea cow.

All species, and in particular the specialized ones—the queer ones—are treasure houses from which man will increasingly draw understanding. In the very *complexity* of the animal lies its great value. No team of engineers, no matter how great the research budget, will ever duplicate a single whisker of a sea cow.

If we think of whales, not as unique systems, but simply

as packages of oil and protein, we can get along nicely without them. We can fish for food in the sea at lower trophic levels. Where we now take a pound of whale we can take a thousand pounds of the microscopic plants which represent that pound of flesh. But we will be eating sea fodder, and it will taste like grass, and it will be costly to gather. It will not come to us in the wholesale, bargain size of the fifty-ton whale.

The world population of blue whales has dropped in thirty years from *one hundred thousand to one thousand*. The blue whale is commercially extinct. By the early 1960s some species of whales were being overkilled in the northern hemisphere as well as in the southern, and now four species in the north are being caught faster than they can reproduce: the blue, humpback, fin, and sperm. Only three nations are still in the business of pelagic whaling: Japan, the Soviet Union, and Norway, and it is doubtful whether any one is making a profit. The average size of whales in the catch is declining, which points suspiciously to overkilling. The CDW—take per catcher's day's work—which is a measure of the effort required to take a whale, is also steadily declining, which tells us what we already know, that the whales are disappearing. The annual take of whales in the Antarctic has been hovering around fifteen thousand units. If the whales are to survive, it will have to be cut to two thousand for many years.

Only international agreement and action can restore the situation. But nations are suspicious and jealous. The larger ones are dominated by military-industrial cores of power. Though legal provision for inspection of each other's whaling activities was made in 1963, the individual nations have been reluctant to act in the spirit of that law.

One slim source of optimism lies in the idea proposed in

A P R I L

1966 by John Gulland of the Department of Fisheries, United Nations Food and Agricultural Organization (FAO). The Gulland plan would place responsibility for the whales in the United Nations, and specifically in an International Whaling Authority. The strength of the Authority would rest on three provisions: annual kill quotas by species, annual kill quotas by nations, and inspection by the Authority. The quotas would rest on research, and the whole scheme would rest on education and goodwill and world-wide reverence for Life. . . . Are we ready for the Gulland plan?

MAY

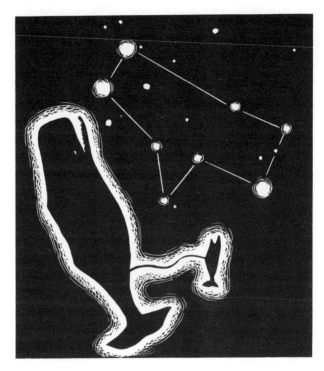

THE Little Calf is now eight months old. A human child at this age is trying to lift its body from the floor, to cling briefly to chairs, and to reach for the hem of mother's skirt. The Little Calf, by contrast, is well along the road to independence; if his mother were to disappear overnight he might perhaps survive alone.

The Little Calf and his mother are feeding four hundred miles at sea off San Francisco. They will go no farther north

MAY

this year, though many of their companions have dropped from sight over the horizon, far on their way to the Bering Sea. The females that came into heat have dallied behind. The pattern of the herd as the Little Calf knew it in spring is dissolving. Whales of like age and sex and breeding disposition are now consorting; the groups are separating in space because of the differences in their swimming speeds.

The day is mild. A filmy diffusion pales the blue of the sky and gives a soft extra light. A gentle breeze touches the moving sea. Here and there the surface breaks in a pattern of light, struck by a shower of needles. Schools of sauries, each holding a million fish, break and boil to the top. Their sides are gleaming iridescent silver; their backs are metallic blue-green. The Little Calf and his mother, along with seven other females, the harem bull, and a young male, are lazily following the fish, feasting as they go. During the bright of day, when the schools descend for reasons of their own—reasons unknown to man— the old whales pursue them down, while during the night the young whales plunge with open jaws through the silver masses. Even the Little Calf, though nursing, is swallowing the fat, tasty, ten-inch fish.

At 9:43 in the morning the silver aircraft *Clipper Dawn*, en route from San Francisco to Honolulu, appears low down in the eastern sky and begins to chalk a clean white line across the blue-black vault.

And at 9:43 a whale in the family of the Little Calf is in distress.

For several weeks the Little Calf has been aware of two

grown females in the family who are traveling together at the edge of the group. Their bellies are rounded, especially the belly of one. She is, in fact, the youngish female who carries the two-foot length of swordfish bill embedded in her hump. She is about to give birth to her first calf, and all is not going well. On either side of her lower belly the outline of a breast shows clearly as an oval pad, five feet long. Her navel bulges like a white fist. She is tense, irritable, clumsy. She bends her long trunk and tail at right angles to her body and whips them back again. The slit of her vagina flares pink from time to time. The taut outer profile of her flank changes visibly, rippling and bulging as the fetus changes position in her womb.

When she slows her swimming speed and begins to twist near the surface of the sea, four other whales move in, drawn by an excitement as old as life itself. A young male, puzzled, or perhaps annoyed, by the strange behavior of the female, butts her rudely under the left flipper and she brings the limb down with a stunning blow across his eye. The whales circle the female, talking in ultrasound and giving also the rare, shrill buzz, audible to man, which springs from the blowhole with a stream of bubbles. The young mother-to-be is breathing heavily.

At 9:53 the gray folded tail flukes of a calf appear at the birth opening, then retreat. They slowly reappear. The mother contorts her body to the limit of its bulky shape and jerks her tail convulsively. The gray-and-black infant slides out rapidly until the flippers are due to come. (At this level of the baby's

MAY

body the girth is greatest, or about what a man could circle with his arms.) Here the flippers catch in the opening; the body hangs. The little thing is now clearly a male.

Minutes pass. The mother twists and the calf twists, though his movements grow slower and more feeble. The pair rise and fall in the gentle sea. At 10:46 the mother, still submerged, makes a deep contraction and expels her breath. Instantly the calf is hidden in a cloud of pink. Now he is clear, swimming actively. The mother whirls. The cord stretches and snaps near her belly. In less than a minute the calf is at the surface gasping for air. The muscles of the mother's belly stiffen and contract; the placenta is expelled. She ignores it. (Were she a land mammal she might have eaten it. Land creatures do this, it is said, to destroy an odorous thing which could attract predators to the nest or den and also to restore to the mother some of the nutrients spent in pregnancy.) For an hour blood dribbles from the new mother.

Up above, on the breezy surface of the ocean, the black backs of the whales continue to circle. A score of shearwaters are drawn to the scene, the first of millions now winging their way northward from the nesting season in Bass Strait and among the Islands of Magellan. They skim on rakish black wings only inches above the water, back and forth above the whales. Finding no food, they wheel about and press toward their rendezvous in the sea pastures of Alaska. Soon the Little Calf will see ten thousand birds a day coursing above his feeding grounds.

One hour and three minutes the mother whale was in labor. Though her calf was born early in the season and was slow in coming, he seems to be normal and healthy. He swims now beneath her tail and searches blindly for the nipples. The mother touches him often and tenderly with her sensitive flipper but makes no effort to help him find the place. His right flipper is still crimped from confinement in the womb; he swims lamely. When he strays off into the blue dimness his mother is quickly at his side, nudging him gently. She is a new creature, active, responsive, a ton lighter in weight. Not until evening, when the shadow of the great form beside him is growing vague, does her calf find the soft place on her belly which will be the focus of his waking hours for two years to come.

⚕⚕⚕

ONCE, on a visit to a whaling ship, I had a chance to acquire a rare specimen: a sperm-whale fetus only four inches long. I took the little creature, packed in ice cubes, to the mainland. At my hotel I bought a pint of vodka and a bottle of shaving lotion. I mixed these in a washbasin, slit the belly and chest of the fetus with a razor blade, and embalmed it overnight in the fragrant solution. Later I dissected it in my laboratory.

The fetus had few of the full-grown whale exaggerations in shape. It had, rather, the simple form of a mass of clay newly in the hands of a sculptor. Though the head of the adult is one-third the length of the body, that of the fetus was less than one-quarter. The fetus was tapered like a porpoise, or maybe like the unknown common ancestor of porpoise and whale. In profile, the little head could even have belonged to an infant pig, with eyes shut, lower jaw protruding beyond the snout, and nostrils at the front.

At this stage of development there are two unmistakable nostrils. Later, the right one will close and disappear; the left one will migrate to the top of the head. The head itself will swell and finally blend with the body proper, thus erasing an early suggestion of a neck. On each side of the fetus body, the flipper is a rounded paddle with five distinct ridges representing fingers; the forearm and upperarm bones are extremely short; the whole appendage is a stiff though somewhat elastic vane with a joint movable only at the shoulder socket. It can have no value as a swimming organ except as a hydrofoil to change the direction of travel.

Those parts of the body which in adult life sink beneath the surface of the skin for streamline effect were still visible on the little fetus. The penis protruded; the rudimentary nipples were evident; even the ears were there—tiny ridges of skin, most unfitting for a whale. There were actually traces of whiskers, casting a long shadow from an ancestor dead now forty million years.

〰〰〰

WHILE the Little Calf and his mother are feeding in the eastern Pacific, six hundred men on latitude Forty North, off the main island of Honshu, Japan, are busy with some of his older relatives. Three weeks ago the floating factory *Sonan Maru* sailed from Oshima to intercept the sperm-whale migration moving northward from the tropics. Now she is floating on the high seas. She is the central figure in a vast, round-the-clock operation designed to harvest fifteen hundred sperm whales and nine hundred whales of other species before she turns back to the homeland in November.

The *Sonan* is a greasy, dirty black ship of twenty thousand tons, which is fed continuously with whales by fourteen catcher boats. She has six decks below the water line and three above. On her boat deck is a fleet of transports, small shuttle boats, to take the fresh whale meat to the refrigerator ship nearby. Each transport can haul fifteen tons. When the icy caverns of this "reefer" ship are filled, she will sail for Japan to unload. Until she returns, the *Sonan* will preserve the daily inflow of meat by canning it.

Learning the facts of pelagic whaling on the *Sonan* is Toshio Nakajima, aged twenty-two, a biologist from the Whales Research Institute of Japan. He watches with excitement the vessels coming and going, the workmen crawling over the slippery carcasses with spiked rubber boots, at times only inches from death as the steel blocks and cables swing above their heads. He sees the jets of white steam spurting from strange metal boxes and cylinders and pipes. Day and night he smells the sharp, raw vapors of meat and entrails and bubbling oil, mingled with the rich aroma of whale stew on a giant scale. Day and night he hears the noises of the factory contained in the steel hull of the ship: the hiss of escaping air, the roar of the diesel jets that feed the boilers, the protesting screech of winches, the clear clang of metal on metal, the shouts of workmen—and underneath all the steady throb of the ship as she keeps her nose to the wind, dead slow ahead. Nakajima has learned to ignore the noises; he sleeps at night the sleep of the weary worker.

He is the newest and the greenest of a group—two biologists, a veterinarian, and three inspectors—assigned to the *Sonan* for the whaling season. There is also an "American observer," who watches proceedings from the shelter of a steel cubbyhole where his skull is safe from accident, though at any time his face may stop a gob of flying blubber.

This May morning is a good one for observation. Business is slack; the sea is calm; the sky is bright-hazy, just right for photography.

"Unless another catcher comes in soon," says Nakajima, "the foreman will let us weigh this whale. We haven't had time up to now."

As he speaks, the body of a bull sperm is rising, tail first, through a huge door in the stern of the ship. A "whale claw" at the end of a cable is pulling the black form out of the sea, up a slanting slipway lubricated by gushing hoses. The loudspeaker blares (in Japanese): "Whale number six-o-two on the slip!" As the whale comes to rest on the butchering deck, Nakajima and his partner stretch a tape beside it. They measure its length at fifty feet, five inches. The workmen watch idly. They are not concerned, since the animal is clearly longer than the legal minimum; no one will be blamed this time by the inspector.

At once the butchers start to work, while Nakajima scribbles on a pad of waterproof paper. He notes the usual parasites: the "whale lice" (small crustaceans) crawling on the belly, and the "dead man's fingers" (stalked barnacles) on the back. These pale, fleshy creatures writhe like Gorgon hair. Seconds before the cable starts to rip the whale apart, Nakajima scrapes a sample of diatom film from the whale's back and leaps to safety in the scuppers. *Whi-i-ish!* The belly is laid open and the stomach contents spill on the deck in a gray steaming flood. Nakajima's partner sees a squid that he does not recognize. He tosses it into a pail to be pickled later in formalin. The biologists make a quick, ghoulish raid on the lower regions in search of parasitic worms. With butcher knives they loosen the testes and plop them into a sack. (Next winter in Tokyo they will slice the elliptical glands and look for microscopic evidence of sex activity.) Finally, they approach the great grinning head and with mallet and chisel dislodge two of the upper teeth complete with clinging jawbone and gum. (Next winter they will section the teeth and count the annual rings.)

"*Ai-yai!*" A workman slashing at the belly pauses and looks ruefully at the edge of his blade, then kicks at a hard object in the stomach contents. It is a rough, shaly rock about the size of a brick. Perhaps it was in a halibut or other bottom-fish that was eaten by the whale. Perhaps the whale scooped it up by accident as he jerked the body of an octopus from a submarine ledge.

The foreman signals for a halt. He explains to the workmen that this whale is to be cut into pieces and weighed, bit by bit, on a platform scale. The men laugh and go to work on a project that represents a small break in the drudgery of a whaler's life. The heart comes out separately, and then the lungs, the tongue, and many odd-shaped chunks of meat and bone and blubber. Thirty-two pieces are dragged, one by one, across the slippery deck to the scale, hoisted up, and dragged away again.

From the draining heart, Nakajima fills a blood-sample bottle the size of his thumb and takes it to the ship's coldroom. (Next winter a specialist will type the plasma contained therein and will identify the "genetic tag" carried by this whale. Eventually, students of whale migration will describe the distribution of the various stocks and administrators will assign a whaling quota to each stock.)

An hour later, the tail flukes slap on the scale, marking the end of the job. Meanwhile, a catcher has arrived with two sei whales and another sperm. Most of the crew turn back to the routine. The biologists total up the weight of the whale at forty metric tons (forty-four American tons), not counting the blood and juices that ran in rivulets during the operation.

After lunch the second sperm is butchered. Men with broad, long-handled knives slash deftly around the head. A man on either side fastens a steel hook in the blubber. The winch operator sees that the hooks are fast and, without waiting for a signal, begins to peel back the long strips of white blubber as he would peel a banana. Stony barnacles pop from the skin and drop clattering to the deck. The flensers hack the dark red meat into chunks and push them into a chute which carries them to the transport bobbing alongside. Ten minutes later the small boat speeds off to the refrigerator ship a half-mile away and another takes her place in the shadow of the mother ship. All the while, slabs of blubber are dropping to a lower deck where they move into revolving cookers, to be rendered into oil.

This is butchering indeed! A chain-saw gang attacks the fifty-foot skeleton and minutes later it is in the cookers. The half-acre deck is bare except for a flabby, steaming mound of liver—about a thousand pounds. The liver disappears into the maw of a chute on its way to a special cooker in which the vitamins will be preserved, and men begin to hose down the deck.

On the water fifty feet below the butchering deck, white gulls scream and rage, settling on and rising from the coils of whale intestine that twist and bob gracefully in the wash. They make a pleasing picture in iridescent pink and violet, rimmed in black from the loom of the black hull above.

Not a man has been hurt in all the crowd of men moving on collision courses, many with six-foot knives or power saws. Even the sudden shifting of a strip of meat could crush a man's life, were he not alert to the total scene.

M A Y

The catcher boats attached to the *Sonan* are modern vessels of nine hundred tons displacement and a top speed of seventeen knots. At midnight, one of them, *Seki Maru No. 15*, with the American observer aboard, casts off and heads through the misty night toward a position forty-five miles northwest, where the helicopter pilot from the mother ship reported last evening that he had seen several dozen whales, species undetermined. Toward dawn, she drops to half speed to wait for daylight.

Whale hunting is not glamorous. It is a steady grind in which the gunner does his job and tries to keep from getting hurt. The *Seki* must take at least two sperm whales a day during the peak of the season in order to meet her quota. Once in a while, though, something unusual happens. The harpoon goes clear through one whale and explodes in another, or the gunner doesn't see a calf and kills a nursing mother by mistake. (This is recorded against him, and he gets no pay for the kill.) Each gunner constantly tries to improve his aim so as to hit squarely on the first shot and not need to fire a second or third to kill the whale. Even one harpoon makes trouble for the factory. The soft iron head blows fragments into the flesh, which dull the flenser's knife and carry bits of entrails into the good meat, speeding the process of putrefaction.

Forty feet above the water, three lookouts now take their stations in the swaying crow's nest, while the gunner moves to the bow. He lifts the cover from the 90-millimeter gun and checks the load but keeps the barrel in locked position. He speaks into a chest microphone hidden under his windbreaker and gets an answering "okay" from the bridge. All systems are GO. Wispy skeins of morning mist drift across the path of the vessel.

Soon a hail comes from the microphone in the crow's nest. "Kujira! Kujira!" ("Whale! Whale!") The lookouts have spotted a group of six sperm whales and the chase is on full speed. For a good five minutes the *Seki* seems to be making no headway, or even falling behind. The animals are sprinting at fifteen to twenty knots. Then the gap between hunter and prey begins to narrow. The ship drops to half speed and finally stops. She glides ahead swiftly and quietly, the green water curling cleanly from her prow. The gunner picks a target, the largest animal in the group. He unlocks the weapon and aims at a point where he can see the dark form beneath the surface five seconds before it rises. As the whale blows a geyser through its forehead and is about to dive, the cannon booms and the two-hundred-pound harpoon buries its head in the beast's soft hump. The nylon leader pays out swiftly from a coil in front of the gun as the whale plunges in pain.

The leader is followed by a heavier line which in turn is checked by a massive steel spring. The tackle passes underneath the platform. The gunner will not, like Ahab, be dragged to his death in a wild loop of line.

The whale makes a last powerful surge through reddening waters and a fountain of blood bursts from its back.

Meanwhile, five men hurry to the gun with a fresh harpoon, black powder for the head, and a new shell for the chamber. With extreme care they make ready for another shot in case it should be needed.

It is not, and soon the gunner calls for a back-haul on the line. A one-hundred horsepower winch takes up the slack, and within minutes the whale is alongside. It gives a last great gasping sigh and its flippers jerk in death. The air hose comes into play, a line is looped securely around the tail, and a buoy with a flag and a radio beacon is dropped over the side.

Gulls have dropped to the water beside the whale and are bobbing for clotted blood. The *Seki* resumes the hunt; she will recover this whale later in the day. Just twenty-seven minutes have elapsed since it was first sighted.

The *Seki* continues in the direction taken by the sperm whales, which are now thoroughly alarmed, but when a fog bank moves across the horizon the captain turns on a ninety-degree course. "Last season," he tells the American observer, "we averaged five hours hunting for every whale we took."

"Couldn't you save time if the mother ship had a spotting airplane?" asks the observer.

"Well, of course, she has a helicopter, but the radius of observation is short. Our big shore-whaling station at Abashiri has been using an airplane for more than ten years. It flies usually at five hundred feet and covers a thousand miles a day in good weather. It saves the company a lot of money."

"I've heard that the moon has an influence on hunting success," the observer suggests.

The captain looks at him obliquely. "It's true of sperm-whale hunting. We find the whales in larger groups at *new* moon and *full* moon. No one knows why, though."

On the following day the *Seki* returns to the factory ship with her catch of three whales: two sperms and a finback. The observer, after a nap and a shower, visits the veterinarian, Namkung, a middle-aged Korean who spent five years in a Presbyterian mission and later studied for his profession in the University of Tokyo. Namkung's halting English and a common scientific language enable them to discuss whale diseases and the sanitary aspects of whale-meat production.

"I find difficulty," says Namkung, "in explaining to our people who eat whale meat throughout the year that parasitic worms are okay. Every whale has them. The sperm whale has twenty different kinds. Most of them live in the food tube and the heart and lungs. One time I collected over a hundred pounds of roundworms from the first stomach of a sperm, and they were doing no harm at all, just lying there sharing the whale's food.

"We don't get many pregnant sperm whales this far north but in every one I have cut open I have found the big worm" —he stretches his arms—"that lives only in the placenta. Every food product made from the whale is cooked or sharp-frozen or heavily salted before anyone eats it. The worms are killed, and they're just as good as the meat."

The observer agrees and describes a recent word battle in America over the sale of "fish protein concentrate" (FPC). This is a clean, white, cheap, nutritious food, which was developed by a fishery agency. A farm bureau became jealous and tried to keep it from being sold. It was, said a bureau official, "unwholesome" because it contained the entrails of the fish. On cross-examination the official admitted that he himself had many times eaten with pleasure canned sardines prepared from the whole fish.

"You will perhaps agree," suggests Namkung, "that even if people were to eat raw whale meat they would run little risk? As a rule, wild-animal parasites don't like people and will not stay in them long. The worms are particular—they are 'host specific.' I have looked inside many thousands of whales and they were very healthy. Maybe five or six times I have seen a whale that would not meet the standard for use as food, and in every case it was one that carried an old harpoon injury. Whales must be healthy, because they live so long."

"How do you know they live long?" the observer asks.

"Well, our Japanese hunters in the Antarctic have recovered markers that were shot into sperm whales by the *Discovery* investigators thirty years before. From the teeth of those whales of known age we get the key that unlocks the age of all other sperm whales. The dolphin Pelorus Jack followed ships along New Zealand for thirty-two years, and nobody knows how old he was when he first took up the sport."

"How about radioactivity?" the observer wants to know. "Do you have any evidence that fallout is concentrated in the bodies of whales and eventually passed on to people in whale meat?"

"The Japanese," says Namkung quietly, "are very conscious of this possibility; perhaps more conscious than any other people on earth. But strontium-90 is being built into the bones of every living person all over the world and will be carried in the bodies of our children's children."

🌊🌊🌊

THE *Reports* of the Whales Research Institute include an article on whale meat in Japanese markets, which contains some intriguing recipes. A kind of "sashimi" is made from sliced raw whale meat marinated in rice-wine vinegar. A big, rich hunk of meat is boiled with bitter-orange juice, or ginger soy, or soy with grated radish. Many parts of the whale are canned with flavoring and sold as "yamatomi." A counterpart of hunter's grilled steak, that rough-and-ready standby of the Boy Scouts, is "karibayaki" of whale.

The article states: "The intestines of animals are in general long, so they are called 'hyakuhiro' in Japanese which is meant by [sic] a hundred fathoms. Especially the intestines of whales are long and big, and they are welcomed as a sign of enlarging. This is why the Nagasaki people have used to eat the whale intestines in honour of the New Year."

Whale products were fed experimentally to eight thousand Japanese school children in a test of their likes and dislikes. Whale bacon with cabbage, buns stuffed with minced liver, and many other dishes were offered. The investigators found that boys were more tolerant of strange foods than girls; older children than younger. Children from "economical" districts were more tolerant than those from "luxury" districts.

For "economical," read *poor;* the kids are hungrier there.

The problem of "humaneness" in the chasing and killing of whales troubles me. Dr. H. R. Lillie, a physician who worked with the British whaling fleet in the Southern Ocean, reported: "The method still used in killing whales today is antiquated and horrible. . . . In one extreme case that I witnessed, five hours and nine harpoons were required to kill a female Blue Whale in advanced pregnancy."

As for the so-called blood sports involving deer, rabbits, squirrels, and other land animals, I acknowledge, as a biologist, that *some* method must be used to keep their populations under control.

I think of vivisection and of all the children whose lives have been saved by information it has yielded. But what about the black market in stolen cats and dogs to supply the vivisectionists? I think of the ritual slaughter of food animals by religious sects; of the killing of sea birds by waste oil discharged at sea. I think of filthy roadside zoos; of the battery system of producing eggs and broilers; of animals shot forever into space for purposes of research.

Then I turn to Albert Schweitzer's autobiography:

"I buy from natives a young fish eagle . . . in order to rescue it from their cruel hands. But now I have to decide whether I shall let it starve, or kill every day a number of small fishes, in order to keep it alive. I decide on the latter course, but every day I feel it hard that this life must be sacrificed for the other on my responsibility. Standing, as he does, with the whole body of living creatures under the law of this dilemma . . . man comes again and again into the position of being able to preserve his own life and life generally only at the cost of other life. If he has been touched by the ethic of Reverence for Life, he injures and destroys life only under a necessity which he cannot avoid, and never from thoughtlessness. So far as he is a free man he uses every opportunity of tasting the blessedness of being able to assist life and avert from it suffering and destruction."

JUNE

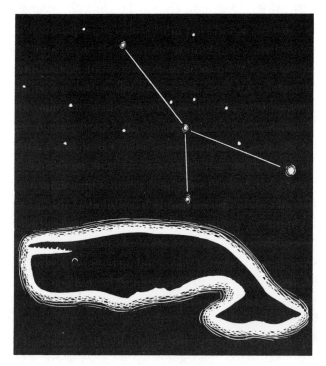

Early in June the Little Calf, still with his mother on the western side of the broad Pacific Ocean, is swimming slowly, approaching with caution a large floating mass that echoes "whale" but yet not the kind of whale he knows. He moves toward the quiet thing. It rises and falls, inert. He turns his snout to right and left, bringing into play all senses. (Mother has moved along a hundred yards.) There it lies—gray, speckled with white. One long flipper dips into the sea and the other stands rakishly in the air like a last call for help. The open belly is a thicket of trailing tissues and, through the tissues, three sleeper sharks wind back and forth with cold eyes, tearing now and then as appetite urges. The thing is a dead humpback whale. It is sixty feet long, toothless like all of its kind, and also eyeless, because swimming crabs have chewed the lenses from their sockets. The great carcass is barely awash. Soon a shark will puncture the arching back and then the thing will settle imperceptibly to the bottom. There a hundred blind scavengers of a hundred sizes will penetrate its flesh and leave at last a skeleton. The hard, white, stony ear bones, the size of a man's fist, will persist for a few decades. Perhaps at last a scientific boat, a deep-sea dredger, will haul these curious bones to the top, though probably the chance is very remote.

A pair of dolphins—harlequins in black and white, perfect in form and splendid in motion—approach the Little Calf. They leap full fifteen feet into the blue, throwing a haze of crystal sparks. To the Little Calf, they are part of the world. They wave and twist ahead in rushing flight, joyous.

Softly the Little Calf sinks. He has no limits. He is in balance with time and space. Infinite time and planetary space are nothing. He stares sleepily into the soft blue growing darker blue and purple black. The pressure gains. He stops. He moves a lazy tail and gently rises to the top. He breathes a dozen drafts.

An hour later, he is loafing near the bright top of the sea. He has filled his belly again with warm, yellow milk and now

J U N E

he tugs gently at the tail of a large fish, a mahimahi, that protrudes from mother's mouth. Is she deliberately teaching him
to take solid food? This is doubtful. At any rate, he tears off a
delicious chunk of white meat and gulps it down.

An hour after sunset the mother of the Little Calf arches
her back and begins her first descent of the day to the deeper
feeding layers. Tonight is her lucky night, for in less than a
minute she finds herself at the edge of a cloud of luminescent
squids. What they lack in size they make up in number; thousands upon thousands of blue-white shapes darting swiftly
through the dark. Turning and twisting blindly she seizes a
dozen elusive forms in her mouth and crushes them to a mass.
She relaxes. Some of the glowing phosphorescent slime from
their skin spreads over the lining of her mouth and clings to
her teeth and tongue. She slides quietly through the sea.
Squids, and the predatory fishes which pursue them, are attracted to the pale cavern of her mouth and, as they come
within range, she bites them easily. When she rises at last to
blow and belch, the Little Calf is there at the surface to greet
her. He is excited by the ghostly fire that gleams from the angle of her jaws, for he has seen it before and he associates it
with food. On her next dive he follows her uncertainly down.

In the meanwhile, the squids have moved up to within a
hundred feet of the surface, where they are now feeding on
plankton. Hugging his mother's flank, the Little Calf sees a
submarine world at night as a dim shadowy mist pierced by
jerking blobs of light. He seizes a pale fragment that curls from
his mother's mouth and finds it good. His excitement grows.

He cleaves the water in a surge of power and his toothless jaws clamp firmly on two of the squids. Now his lungs are feeling the strain and he moves upward. Up and down he travels for a long while, feeding and breathing, making four round trips to his mother's one.

Quite suddenly he is full. He floats at the surface under the stars, drifting now into sleep and then briefly out to move a flipper idly and bring his nostril into the cool sea breeze. Toward daybreak his mother approaches and tests him with the quiet humming of her inner voice. She retreats. For the first time in his short life the Little Calf will not awaken for his morning milk.

ᔕᔕᔕ

THE *Sea Otter* is a small government patrol vessel, which carries wardens and biologists, with their gear, back and forth along the Aleutian Islands throughout the year. As she bobbed at anchor off the southern shore of Amchitka Island one day in June, a weather-beaten mate leaned on the after rail watching a yellow buoy. Down below the surface in the cold water of the North Pacific, "Sea Otter" Hansen, a biologist for the bureau of fisheries, was exploring the bottom in a self-contained diving suit. For twenty years Hansen has guarded the wildlife treasures of Amchitka Island Refuge, forsaking all worldly pleasures for love of the place.

In the course of his routine patrol on foot along the seashore in winter, now crunching on the cobble itself and now clawing his way around a steep headland, Hansen had been finding a great many dead and dying sea otters. Especially after storms he came upon their soggy bodies and white skeletons among the boulders. He weighed and autopsied the fresh carcasses and found them emaciated and riddled with parasites. He decided that something was very wrong with the submarine pastures of Amchitka. Had the sea otters outgrown their food supply? Had a benevolent government carried the "refuge" idea too far? Were the animals within the refuge dying of overprotection, of well-intended kindness?

He decided to investigate the sea bottom. Leaning against the current in a watery blue vault of the ocean, he groped in a wet suit on a five-fathom bottom with a netting sack in his left hand. He was sampling the organisms that grow on the bottom, testing his theory that food is scarce and poor in quality. He picked a green sea urchin, a spiny ball the size of his fist, and then a chiton, a leathery boat-shaped mollusk that clings stubbornly to its rocky bed. Orange, brown, and red starfishes he passed by, for they are unimportant; only a starving sea otter will turn to these gritty things for sustenance. Into his bag he thrust black sea mussels and rock oysters, tiny snails that he calls "periwinkles," hairy snails, moon snails, crabs, tube worms, and clams. His fingers were turning blue with cold; he was about to call it quits and swim back to the ship. Later, in his warm laboratory, he would study the specimens, though already he was sure that they were stunted and sparse. Few of them had had a chance to mature and reproduce; most of their companions were taken away weeks ago, half-grown, by hungry sea otters.

Suddenly the light changed. Shark! he thought, and then his panic ebbed; there are no man-eating sharks in these sub-arctic waters. Killer whale! Panic surged again. He clung to a stalk of kelp and leaned backward, staring above him. No more than ten feet from his mask a great gray form was passing in utter silence, eclipsing the blue light. A whale! But surely not a killer—far too big. It seemed a full minute before the tail flukes glided before his eyes and the curtain of shadow lifted as quickly as it came. Hansen exhaled in a burst of bubbly relief and headed upstream toward the buoy.

Up the rope ladder and on deck, he threw off his tank and mask. "Man!" he cried to the mate. "Did you see that whale?"

"Yep. I didn't sound the buzzer because I knew he wouldn't hurt you. It was a gray. Must be the first of the migration."

The mate was right. The California gray whales, ten thousand strong, were on the move. The vanguards were threading northwest through the Aleutian passes, trailed many miles and many weeks behind by the mothers with their Christmas calves.

One of the old bulls in the lead has followed the route from Mexico to Chukchi Sea for fifty years, a one-way route of four thousand five hundred miles. He slides along through the wastes of water at a steady pace of a hundred miles a day. His long body, burdened with a frost of barnacles, will continue north to the limit of navigation. By August he will be spy-hopping and lob-tailing and breaching among the broken ice cakes of the Arctic Ocean only a thousand miles from the Pole. He will seem to smirk with satisfaction as his dripping head rises from the water and he swallows great balls of orange plankton.

The gray whales, the strange whales, have never crossed the equator. Though now they live only in the North Pacific, their bones have been dug from European sands. They have been found in seacoastal beds deposited in some unrecorded time after primitive man had arrived from Africa. The gray whale comes inshore to breed. Did this habit spell destruction for the European stock? Did hairy hunters in skin boats find out the secret breeding place and kill the last whale there?

SSS

LAST November in the year of the whale the Little Calf's half-sister who was caught for Life Arena had survived the hardships of capture and greedily started swallowing an artificial diet resembling her mother's milk. She was the first sperm whale ever to live in captivity.

Now, half a year later, she is swimming in a measured circle in her green pool; waiting for her morning meal. The staff of the aquarium have named her "Susie" after a slender black-haired girl who has come to Life Arena once or twice a week throughout her high-school career. "Crazy about animals," they say of the girl Susie. She works without pay, feeding the porpoises, scrubbing the glass walls of the fish tanks, and nursing the so-called orphan seals that well-meaning people bring to Life Arena in summer in the delusion that they have been abandoned. Often she simply sits dreamily watching the animals or sketching the attitudes they take.

The moment that Susie saw the young sperm whale sliding through the water, a rapport began to grow between them, a bond stronger than the feeling of the whale for the men in uniform upon whom she depended for food.

Now in June the captive whale has just been weaned from her liquid diet at twenty months or so. (The men at Life Arena try to guess her age.) She may have been weaned too early. She weighs only two tons and is in fact underweight, though on a rich diet of a hundred pounds a day she is fast nearing the normal size of a sperm-whale youngster in the open sea.

Most of her food is opalescent squid, a kind of soft, naked, free-swimming mollusk that swarms in Monterey Bay. Its body, eight inches long, is milky-translucent, faintly bluish, with brilliant blue-green spots that blaze and fade and run in rippling waves along the pale skin. In early summer the squids gather to mate and then to lay their eggs on the sandy rims of the submarine canyons of the Bay. Then the fishermen come at night with lampara nets and purse seines and flashing lights to harvest them by the thousands of tons. Some of the catch is frozen in blocks of ice and trucked to nearby Life Arena, where it is fed to Susie the Whale.

At first she stubbornly refused to eat the squids. Week after week the patient keepers tried to slip the solid food into her gullet at nursing time. She quickly learned their game and jerked away. In desperation they sent a refrigerated tank-truck to the Bay and returned with a thousand living squids which they poured into her pool. At first she was frightened by the flashing forms. Then she began to play with them, snapping her jaws like a dog at a window pane trying to catch blue-bottle flies. At the end of the week, the keepers cut her milk supply in half. Susie the Whale was disturbed. She swam constantly. Then she began to swallow some of the squids whose fleshy forms she had up to now been content simply to crush.

When Susie first learned to feed, she was briefly a television star. A cameraman, sweating with exertion and fright in a rubber suit, followed her around the tank, catching the images of white squids drifting like snow across the dark opening of her mouth. In two dramatic weeks she was weaned from milk to living squids, and then to freshly thawed squids dumped from the keeper's bucket.

Susie the Girl could not keep away from her namesake. But a note from school suggested that perhaps she was neglecting her homework. Reluctantly she turned to the gray world imposed by adults for the two remaining weeks of school.

In the meantime, she had moved far in her groping effort to *reach* the little whale, to strengthen the bond of communication. She had learned to scrub the sensitive snout with a brush. Garbed in a sweatshirt and faded jeans, she had learned to hold a rubber tire and to let the whale struggle with toothless jaws to tear it from her grasp. (The contest was always short and in favor of the whale.) After long deliberation, the manager of Life Arena gave in to her latest bold request: to ride on the back of Susie the Whale.

It proved to be no trick at all. In the open sea, the wild young sperm whales often wrestle with each other (if I may use this word to describe the sliding, rolling, pounding games of body contact they play). So the transfer from whale-against-whale to girl-on-tail really broke no rule in the instinctive code of Susie the Whale. The keeper stood by tensely, boat hook in hand, as the girl slipped into the water. More in excitement than in fear, she pushed her palms against the black flukes. The whale turned half circle in mild surprise, then paused to blow. Spitting water, the girl scrambled to the top of the tapering trunk, gripping the slippery skin with her knees, and rose triumphantly. There she swayed for a long moment, black hair streaming, arms outstretched, a figure from a Cretan vase—twenty-five centuries full circle!

JULY

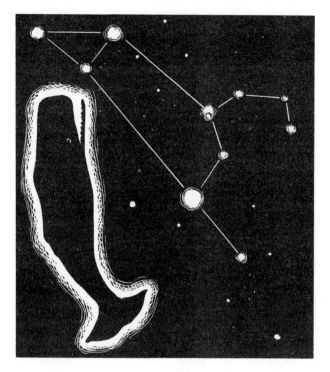

IN the year of the whale there are days when nothing is new. On such a day in July the air is filled with a monotonous hissing of sound as one rain squall pursues another across the dappled sea. The Little Calf swims beneath his mother's body in a dark shadow illuminated at the edges by a blue-gray light from above. Subconsciously he tries to match the rhythmic, undulating sameness of her body, for the beating impulses of her flesh and the surrounding water have been one great throbbing part of his life from its beginning. In trying to keep pace, he sometimes falls behind and must sprint for a dozen strokes to re-enter the comforting zone of shadow. When she pauses to rest near the surface he rubs the corner of his mouth against her nipples to stimulate the flow of milk. Half-asleep, she nurses him for a few minutes, then rouses and moves along. Toward evening, she leaves him in the care of other adults and begins to dive for food.

The year of the whale resembles the year of man a thousand centuries ago, when life was plain and brutish and progress was measured in simple terms of staying alive. Now humans crowd more and more into a single life, ask for excitement to the point of stress, and often go beyond. If, by some magic of electronics, man could spy on the intimate life of a whale, even for a week, he would turn away, bored and restless.

On the next day, the sun shines again and the Little Calf is in playful mood. The family overtakes a drifting set of heavy planks all bound together like a raft—a hatch cover torn by storm from the deck of a steamer in a distant sea. The thing is ten feet square and it rides heavily on the swell. Gooseneck barnacles hang beneath it in the green shade and tirelessly comb the water with their fringes. Tube worms and a dozen kinds of green and brown and red seaweeds trail and twist in the stream, while creatures no larger than matchheads browse like tiny goats among the foliage.

The Little Calf slides beneath the sluggish raft, rubbing

the skin of his back along the brushy texture. He boosts it and enjoys the splash as it falls back. He turns and hits it harder and wallows and tumbles in pleasure and finally flops the thing completely over. Two other young whales join in the sport. They play until exhausted, not as much from muscle tiredness as from overheating. They have no sweat glands. The outer skin and the flippers and the tail surfaces begin to flush and the temperatures rise within the warm coats of insulating blubber until at last the little whales have had enough. All but the Little Calf. He is now eleven months old. In a final rush of spirit he takes off at top speed toward the distant sound of mother's voice and all at once he is a flying whale, airborne for the first time, skimming a full three seconds above the sea in a sparkling shower of light.

He rests beside his mother. Flitting shadows touch his head and he rolls easily to one side to look upward. The source of the shadows is gone already down the line of vision. Clean white birds beat the air with rhythmic, tireless wings. Seven arctic terns, streamer-tailed relatives of the gulls, speed to their nesting grounds at the tundra edge of melting snow. Ten thousand miles they wing their way from Antarctic to Arctic in the northern summer and ten thousand miles return in fall. All this on a few ounces of fuel—an incredible voyage.

Their frail bodies are buffeted by wind, but they move on a steady course toward the north. They pause to rest every thousand miles or so, dropping lightly to flotsam on the water, to a log or a raft of kelp. (They hesitate to wet their breasts on the sea itself.) Soon they will reach a gravel beach along a wild clean Alaskan stream and there they will lay their eggs on the bare rocks.

The Little Calf also knows the other terns—the sooty terns. Now in July these handsome black-and-white relations of the arctic tribe are nesting a million strong on oceanic islands of the Pacific. I write of the sooty terns with great wonder, for they stay aloft for months on end, with no cushion but the air, or such, at least, is the evidence. Men do not see the terns at rest outside the breeding season, and, what is more, the feet and feathers of the birds do not seem well adapted for life on the sea. I tire to think of their tireless circles far above the world.

ϑϑϑ

WHEN the Little Calf is resting does he fall asleep? Again I think about the meaning of words, for "sleep" is a man-word. Do the collective quiet times of a sperm whale resemble man's third-of-the-day in bed, turned to blackouts and dreams and scattered rational thoughts? Surely not. Dolphins, at least, never seem to sleep in the usual sense. They rest in a semitorpid state in the water but rarely close both eyes.

Time and again I have read of ships colliding with sperm whales. The usual interpretation (so entered in the ship's log) is "we struck a sleeping whale." But I do not think that whales ever sleep in the human way, for throughout life they must rise at intervals to the surface to breathe, or else consciously maintain their specific gravity (by changing the volume of air in the lungs) so as to remain at the surface.

The rule of life for cetaceans is: bob up and down or die. And when a whale dies, it dies suddenly. When it goes into coma it sinks into the water and is cut off at once from life-giving air. This poses a special problem for the experimental biologist trying to anesthetize a cetacean for study. A few whales and porpoises have been immobilized in the wild, though, sadly, they have also stopped breathing. No way of restarting their respiration has been found.

Only through a complicated maneuver in the laboratory can the feat be accomplished. A porpoise is strapped to an operating table and is tranquilized to reduce its struggling. Then an operator with small, sensitive hands, slips a rubber hose through the mouth into the breathing canal. He introduces an anesthetic and starts a respirator which begins to pump rhythmically, thus breathing for the animal during its unconsciousness. The patient survives to swim away in its pool.

Vagn Flyger of the Natural Resources Institute, University of Maryland, with Eskimo companions, once tried to immobilize a white whale in the Arctic Ocean by shooting it with a projectile syringe. The operation went beautifully at first. The syringe buried itself in the back muscles and discharged its load of drugs. The startled whale dove immediately but reappeared in thirty seconds and lay motionless at the surface, only its tail twitching. Flyger was elated.

At this point there was enacted one of those short dramas that can break a biologist's heart. An excited Eskimo, seeing only a splendid target at close range, raised his rifle and fired, killing the whale and ending the experiment.

𝓰𝓰𝓰

THE eastern limit of the sea pasture in which the Little
Calf and his family are feeding today is the coastal strip of central California. This humid strip is the habitat or native haunt
of a peculiar race of men who see in any new event, in any
change of circumstance, a potential source of dollar revenue.
They speak of the "fast buck," though only to members of their
own kind. To others they speak of "opportunity," "advance-
ment," "progress," or "improvement." Each member of the
race has an angle. His delight is to guess the other's angle
while concealing his own.

All this sets the stage for a certain July event.

During the night, a dead sperm whale floats on a flood
tide to a beach north of the Golden Gate. It is a small whale,
only twenty-two feet long. It comes to rest in a fog. No one
knows it is there until a beachcomber, searching for glass balls
and odd bits of driftwood, sees the dark thing in the surf at four
in the morning. He rubs his eyes, then runs to a seaside cafe
that serves early breakfast to the perch fishermen. He calls his
friend McGill. McGill is a member of the special race. He runs
a tourist trap at Sausalito. It sits beside the road, and its on-and-
off red light should be a warning to navigators of the road but
instead it lures them in. Here they buy souvenirs of the West
(made in Japan and Czechoslovakia). They buy delicate carv-
ings on genuine simulated ivory depicting an Eskimo pressing
his sledge dogs to the limit (made ten at a time with a master

template and a routing machine in a Market Street basement).

McGill rouses from sleep and gets the message. At once alert, his eyes glisten and shift; a fleeting smile crosses his lips. "Be right over," he says as he jumps into his pants. "Get back and stake out a claim on that there whale!"

The beachcomber is paid off with a five-dollar bill and a share of stock in McGill Enterprises (worth perhaps a dollar and a half), and soon McGill himself has the whale on a truck, towing it to Santa Clarissima. Here he bargains with a mortician to embalm it. The mortician, too, is one of the fast-buck race. He telephones to a supplier; he orders more formalin-and-mercury than a respectable undertaker would use in a disaster.

After an all-night operation the whale is rigid. A blue-gray film settles over its eyes and its tongue pulls back in a queer triangle, though no one knows the difference. McGill hoses the body down and covers it with a tarpaulin, then heads for the nearest sign shop.

In just thirty-six hours after it stranded in the haunts of California man, the whale stares into the distance, resting on the truck, while above it a sign proclaims:

BIGGEST LIVING THING ON EARTH   TOUCH IT   FEEL IT
A FULL-GROWN WHALE FROM THE ABISMAL DEPTHS
OF THE SEA   THE LEVIATHAN OF HOLY WRIT
ONE DAY ONLY   ONE DOLLAR

Each night the truck moves in darkness to a roadside stand at the edge of a small town and each morning the flow of visitors begins. The whale is a gold mine. July turns to August, and the thermometer climbs to one hundred and five. An ineffable vapor rises from the patient corpse. When McGill eats a hamburger it tastes like whale and when he eats an egg it tastes like whale. During the day he begins to hate this whale and in his dreams at night he is pursued by whales in great variety, all of which he hates.

The exhibit is shopworn, too. Along its graying sides are carved initials, and the names of motorcycle gangs and schools and lovers and political candidates. The eyes have long since disappeared and a half-dozen teeth have been pried loose behind McGill's back.

When the whiskey, too, begins to taste like whale, McGill is alarmed. He changes the sign to

FOR SALE, YOUR PRICE

but he has no offer. The town marshal suggests that perhaps the whale has outstayed its welcome, though the marshal personally has nothing against a good, clean, educational-type exhibit. McGill has in mind a solution. It is typical of his kind to anticipate a way out, with several good alternatives.

That night he drives a hundred miles to a lookout point on the Palisade Drive. He loosens the fastenings on the whale, backs the truck swiftly to the concrete guardrail and jumps on the brake as the rear tires hit. The truck rears like a frightened mustang and its burden slides into empty space. Ages later (it seems) a distant crash merges with the sound of the booming surf and the whale returns to its primordial home.

AUGUST

THE year of the whale draws to a close. The Little Calf has grown six feet in body length and has gained twelve hundred pounds. He will nurse for another year, though several months before his mother's breasts turn dry he will be feeding largely for himself. His weaning will come about through a mutual loss of interest between mother and calf; she irritated by the butting of the three- or four-ton baby and he annoyed by the trickle of milk that fails to satisfy his surging appetite. The fall season will find mother and calf in waters north of the Hawaiian Islands. The mother will not come in heat this year; she will have no urge to join the noisy harem on the Tropic of Cancer where last September she gave birth to the Little Calf.

In August the sperm whales of the North Pacific are widely scattered from the equator to the Bering Sea. Half of them are south of the Great Circle between southern California and southern Japan, and half are north. This imaginary "half-the-population line" will soon drop south and in March will turn north again.

In the Arctic Ocean, long crooked channels of blue water spread daily between the drifting ice cakes. The limits of the ice retreat toward the Pole. For another month, into September, the edge of the pack will crumble under the rays of the sun. Now if ever is the season when the stout ships of the polar scientists pass from the North Atlantic to the North Pacific, and vice versa, above the continents of the Old World and the New. In September the earth will turn the corner of its path around the sun and the days will shorten. A film of new sea ice will form each night between the floes, and gradually the great white polar sheet will creep south again through the Chukchi Sea and into the Bering.

In August now a solitary sperm whale has reached the northern limit of his range; he is feeding off Cape Navarin at Sixty-two North. The sudden flowering of his breath stands white in the cold air. He sees a solitary iceberg drifting quietly in the last stages of decay, far from the pack, riddled and channeled by sun and rain. At one edge it is stained brown where a walrus family rested a month ago and many miles away. The bull whale rises from a feeding dive with a trail of gray mud clouding the water behind him, for the Bering Sea is shallow here. (The sea floor was dry land thirty thousand years ago, when the first Americans walked across it from Asia.) The bull crowds to the limit of his chilly range, not because it is comfortable but because the food is rich. He finds a wealth of squid and also creatures of the bottom that he rarely feasts on in the North Pacific: crabs, octopus, and dogfish sharks.

At Life Arena, Susie the Girl is working for the summer as a Visitor Guide—her first paid job. Two physiologists from a nearby university have arrived with a mass of equipment: glassware and tubing, metal frames, adhesives, devices with numbered dials, batteries, and a hundred odds and ends. They are planning some experiments on Susie the Whale to get data on how whales keep warm in cold water and how they cool off after they have exercised.

Peter Skansen and John Cantwell have studied heat regulation in animals for many years. They have sweated together in the Mojave Desert, looking at lizards and snakes, and they have shivered together at Cape Crozier, looking at penguins and seals. Most of what they know of heat regulation in whales has been learned by crude methods: pushing thermometers into freshly killed animals at whaling stations; dissecting carcasses. Once a female finback was stranded near John's summer cottage and stayed alive on the beach a day and a half.

They put thermometers into her body openings, and after she died took chunks of fresh tissue to preserve for study. They also experimented by putting blocks of ice into a tank with a porpoise and found that the animal shivered for a while, then, in effect, its body thermostat clicked on. In a few minutes it seemed normal.

Now, having heard that Susie the Whale is partly tamed, they propose to find out what she can tell them—indirectly—about her body heat exchange. They explain their purpose to the manager and the veterinarian of Life Arena, with Susie the Girl listening.

The manager is eager to help. "You know, gentlemen, zoo-keeping is a strange mixture of show business and science. We always have to think of money, expenses, the budget. But we have a real appetite for new ideas about animals. There is no money in zoo-keeping; our satisfaction comes from trying to bring man into sympathy with the animals that outnumber him a million to one. Tell us what we can do for you."

"Well, first, how much do you estimate that Susie weighs?"

"Maybe two tons, and she's eating a hundred pounds a day."

Skansen scribbles on the back of an envelope. "Then I figure she needs about fifteen thousand calories a day, or roughly six times the demand of a man. But this suggests that she's eating too much. Hm-m-m . . . wet food . . . some of it probably lost in the pool . . ."

The questions continue. The scientists learn that Susie

the Whale is most relaxed and least excited by visitors to Life Arena, on Monday mornings. They learn how far Susie the Girl has gone in her effort to reach the whale; to what extent she has been able to manipulate her; what she has accomplished in her attempts to touch sensitive parts like the blowhole and the belly.

Now Pete, grinning, pulls out an FM transmitter from his bag of scientific gear and places it against his own stomach. *Beep-beep-beep* . . . It sounds a clear signal. "I tried this gadget on myself," he says. "I swallowed it after breakfast this morning. It's a remote-sensing thermistor in a capsule about the size of my thumb. I would say that, by now, it's right about here"—pointing.

So on Monday at dawn, Pete and John, Susie the Girl, and a keeper are feeding the little whale. They hide a thermistor in the belly of a herring. Susie the Whale gulps it down without a pause. But she is not so sure that all is well when Susie the Girl slips long metal thermometers into her vaginal opening and her rectum; she is definitely nervous when Susie places a soft rubber cup, like a "plumber's friend," over her blowhole. This breathing pore is the portal of life itself. By a sensitive, palpating, pleading approach to the whale's mouth, Susie succeeds in holding a thermometer under her tongue for thirty seconds, which is long enough for the scientists. Now through the rubber cup on the nostril a sample of gases in and out is being collected.

"Watch out for the loose stuff!" cautions the manager. "We don't want her to swallow any hardware." He knows from long experience that animals in zoos and aquariums will pick up bottles and bottle tops, coins, combs, plastic toys, all the debris that thoughtless visitors toss within their reach.

Susie the Whale is growing restless. She slaps her tail smartly on the surface. She gently seizes the arm of her friend Susie the Girl. The girl is now rubbing the flank of the beast while Pete is trying to draw a blood sample.

But no! the whale is alarmed! She breaks away with wires and rubber tubing in wild disarray. She circles and lifts her body . . . *swoosh!* The scientists are drenched; they laugh. They have, they think, enough data. If any bits are lacking they will try again; perhaps next summer, when their co-worker Susie is back to help them.

The thermistor moving aft in the whale's inner parts keeps up its monotonous *beep-beep-beep*.

ᔕᔕᔕ

MUCH of the work on the physiology of sperm whales stems from a desire to explain their peculiar behavior—how they are able to dive so deep and stay under so long. Scientists are constantly groping for clues in their structure to account for such facts. Their body tissues and organs have been analyzed and compared with what is known of similar cell groups in man and in laboratory animals—dogs and cats, for example.

So far, nothing remarkable has been discovered about whale blood. It has about the same volume in relation to body weight as that of land mammals. The size of the heart also has the same relation to that of the body; in a full-grown sperm whale it weighs from three hundred to four hundred pounds. The heart beats twenty times a minute, but this is reasonable for such a large animal. The aorta is enormous—bigger than a stovepipe—but that too is not surprising in a whale.

The important fact about whale blood in relation to heat regulation is that the whale has parallel systems of blood vessels. Sometimes an artery and a vein lie side by side; in other parts of the body an artery will be surrounded by a ring of small veins, like a TV coaxial cable. In either arrangement, the warm blood flowing out to the skin gives up part of its heat to the returning venous blood and in this way saves the heat from being lost in contact with the cold water. These counter-current systems are found all over the body and seem to work together, under some mysterious control, like traffic systems.

Other factors are also important in heat regulation, a task that is a thousand times greater for a whale resting quietly in a polar sea than for one swimming actively at the equator. First, the whale's body shape is advantageous for this purpose. Whales are all smooth and rounded, with short appendages. This shape, like that of a thermos bottle, conserves heat. So does their layer of insulating blubber, although the blubber is not all for warmth. If it were they would be many times overinsulated. The blubber is also an energy store—theoretically at least, it would enable a large whale to go from four to six months without food. The final factor that aids in conserving heat is the high metabolic rate of cetaceans as compared to land animals. They burn their food rapidly and this too helps to keep them warm.

When ways are found for keeping whalebone whales—

the toothless kinds—in captivity the problem of studying them will be much simpler. Before the Second World War the Japanese succeeded in penning a little piked whale in a bay south of Tokyo. Fish were put in the bay for it, but there was no way to tell whether it ate or not, and after about a month it died. Perhaps a sort of "pellet plankton" food will eventually be developed, something like the packaged food given to goldfish, but much larger.

Porpoises and dolphins are far more manageable than whales—they have been kept successfully in aquariums since 1913, when Charles H. Townsend introduced the first porpoise captured alive to an admiring public at the old New York Aquarium on the Battery.

IN the last week of August the Little Calf and his mother are feeding on the great and deep Pacific, halfway between San Francisco and Oahu, a thousand miles from nearest land. Remote indeed they are, but not lonely, for never are they out of range of the submarine voices of their own kind.

The final day of the year of the whale is a climax to a normal year of life in which adventure is mingled with routine, and stress is intertwined with rest, and food is paced with hunger.

Today at dawn the mother and calf begin to hear again the familiar sounds of their lesser relatives, the porpoises. But now they hear new sounds as well: the steady throb of a tuna ship (a purse seiner) and the echoes bounding from the plump bodies of a thousand tunas—yellowfin and skipjack. The turmoil centers around a fishing scene that the mother could not have known ten years ago, for it is a modern scene. The invention of lightweight nylon netting and powerful hydraulic net-hauling machines has led the fishermen to abandon hand-lining in favor of purse-seining. Now mother and calf see at a distance, but do not comprehend, the capture of a hundred tons of fish in one great sweeping haul.

The blue-gray ship moves swiftly toward a choppy circle of the sea: a sea all torn with the rushing bodies of tunas and porpoises feeding together in a tight group three hundred yards across. The ship circles the melee, assisted by two swift launches that concentrate the animals as a cowboy surrounds the cattle in his charge. A half-mile net is dropped astern, then the ship backs down to let the porpoises, but not the fish, escape. Seven porpoises, though, fail to jump the net; they are confused and frightened; they tangle in the folds and drown. The fishermen chop their sleek bodies from the webbing and drop them over the side. The purse net tightens and the great bright leaping fish, cold-eyed, pour onto the deck. They flail briefly and die, staring. The catch is over in two hours.

As the year ends, the form of the Little Calf leaves a thin track on the flat immensity, a swirling punctuation, a blend of liquid and life. A cool wind moves. The red light gleams on the wave at his brow. Then the sun sinks below the sea, and the tiny whale is gone.

REFERENCE NOTES

SEVEN WHALING CLASSICS: A SELECTED
AND ANNOTATED BIBLIOGRAPHY

INDEX

Reference Notes

PAGE & LINE

v   Henry Beston, *The Outermost House: A Year of Life on the Great Beach of Cape Cod* (2nd ed. New York: Holt, Rinehart & Winston, Inc., 1949), p. 25.

3: 1–4 Stewart L. Udall, "Hope for Earth's Fragile Wildlife," International Union for Conservation of Nature and Natural Resources, *IUCN Bulletin* [Morges, Switzerland], vol. 2 (1966), p. 2.

4: 24–27 Frederick D. Bennett was an English surgeon who went on a whaling voyage in 1833. The quotation is from his *Narrative*, vol. 2, p. 155. The book is described in the Annotated Bibliography (page 206).

5: 11–13 Herman Melville, *Moby-Dick*, p. 131; for a description of the book, see the Annotated Bibliography (page 207).

14: 4–25 This story is based on J. F. G. Wheeler, "Notes on a Young Sperm-Whale from the Bermuda Islands," *Proceedings of the Zoological Society of London*, 1933, part 2, pp. 407–410.

21: 14–19 Henry Lee, *Sea Monsters Unmasked* (London: Wm. Clowes and Son, 1883), p. 2.

21: 22 Alfred, Lord Tennyson, "The Kraken," *The Poems and Plays of Alfred*
through *Lord Tennyson* (New York: Modern Library, 1938), p. 10.
22: 5

28: 20 Arthur F. McBride, *Deep-Sea Research* (London: Pergamon Press, 1956), pp. 153–154. Manuscript notes on evidence of echo-location by porpoises, published by William E. Schevill after McBride's death.

28: 27 William E. Schevill and Barbara Lawrence, "Underwater Listening to the White Porpoise . . . ," *Science*, vol. 109 (1949), pp. 143–144.

29: 14 Schevill and Lawrence, "Food-Finding by a Captive Porpoise," *Breviora*, Museum of Comparative Zoology [Harvard], no. 53 (1956), pp. 1–15.

The Year of the Whale

PAGE & LINE

29: 19   W. N. Kellogg, "Echo Ranging in the Porpoise," *Science,* vol. 128 (1958), pp. 982–988.

32: 3–8   "Swordfish Punctures a Research Submarine," *New Scientist,* January 11, 1968, p. 63.

33: 4   *Aleut* is a fictitious name.

34: 2   *Orchid* is a fictitious name.

35: 22   "Saved by a Porpoise," *Natural History* (New York), vol. 58 (1949),
through   pp. 385–386.
36: 22

36: 24   *Fairy* is a fictitious name.

39: 19   The story of the "convention" is composite, based in part on the real
through   First International Convention on Cetacean Research, in Washington,
43: 10   1963. The results of that symposium were published as: Kenneth S. Norris (ed.), *Whales, Dolphins, and Porpoises* (Berkeley, Calif.: University of California Press, 1966). *My* convention draws on the following:

    Keller Breland, Comment from the floor, *Whales, Dolphins, and Porpoises, op. cit.,* p. 253.

    David K. Caldwell, Melba C. Caldwell, and Dale W. Rice, "Behavior of the Sperm Whale . . . ," *Whales, Dolphins, and Porpoises, op. cit.,* pp. 677–717.

    Arthur F. McBride and D. O. Hebb, "Behavior of the Captive Bottle-Nose Dolphin . . . ," *Journal of Comparative and Physiological Psychology,* vol. 41 (1948), pp. 111–123.

    A. Brazier Howell, *Aquatic Mammals: Their Adaptations to Life in the Water* (Baltimore: Charles C. Thomas, 1930), p. 310.

    Tokuzo Kojima, "On the Brain of the Sperm Whale . . . ," *Scientific Reports of the Whales Research Institute* (Tokyo), no. 6 (1951), pp. 49–72.

    Sam H. Ridgway, N. J. Flanigan, and James G. McCormick, "Brain–Spinal Cord Ratios in Porpoises: Possible Correlations with Intelligence and Ecology," *Psychonomic Science,* vol. 6 (1966), pp. 491–492.

    John Cunningham Lilly, *The Mind of the Dolphin: A Nonhuman Intelligence* (Garden City, N.Y.: Doubleday, 1967).

42: 30   L. Harrison Matthews, "Chairman's Introduction. . . ." *Whales, Dolphins, and Porpoises, op. cit.,* p. 5.

45: 17   *Naval Aviation News,* December 1956, p. 19.

REFERENCE NOTES

PAGE & LINE

46: 16–27   D. F. Eschricht, *On the Species of the Genus Orca Inhabiting the Northern Seas*, 1862; English translation by W. H. Flower in *Recent Memoirs on the Cetacea* (London: Ray Society, 1866), pp. 151–188. The killer whale story was retold in E. J. Slijper, *Whales* (London: Hutchinson, 1962); the quotation is from p. 274 of that book.

48: 8   The tug, which is fictitious, belongs to "Life Arena," an imaginary public aquarium for the display of marine life. Life Arena's functions, described in the following pages and in later chapters, include education and scientific research.

53: 14   The section on the evolution of whales is based in part on Remington
through   Kellogg, "The History of Whales—Their Adaptation to Life in the
57: 17   Water," *Quarterly Review of Biology*, vol. 3 (1928), pp. 29–76, 174–208.

61: 15   The descent of Hannes Keller and Peter Small to 1,000 feet on Decem-
through   ber 3, 1962, was widely publicized in the press. Since then, men have
62: 2   withstood even greater pressures in "simulated dives" in compression tanks on dry land. In 1968, Ralph W. Brauer of Duke University "descended" to 1,197 feet (*New Scientist* [London], July 11, 1968, p. 62).

62: 17   *Search* is a fictitious name.

76: 22   After Julian Taylor told me the story of the ice-locked whales it ap-
through   peared in a scientific journal: R. J. F. Taylor, "An Unusual Record of
77: 3   Three Species of Whale Being Restricted to Pools in Antarctic Sea-Ice," *Proceedings of the Zoological Society of London*, vol. 129 (1957), part 3, pp. 325–331.

77: 22   Romain Gary, *The Roots of Heaven* (New York: Simon and Schuster,
through   1958), p. 61.
78: 7

80: 16–20,   Antony Alpers, *Dolphins* (London: John Murray, 1963), pp. 213, 217,
25–31   220.

83: 17   Ambrose John Wilson, "The Sign of the Prophet Jonah and Its Modern
through   Confirmation," *Princeton Theological Review*, vol. 25 (1927), pp. 635–
84: 18   637.

84: 19–30   Letter of May 18, 1967. Fraser is on the staff of the British Museum (Natural History) and has written many technical papers on whales.

84: 31   Egerton Y. Davis, "Man in Whale," *Natural History* (New York), vol.
through   56 (1947), p. 241.
86: 10

PAGE & LINE

86: 17   The story of the mass stranding is based on D. G. Lillie, "Cetacea,"
through   *British Antarctic ("Terra Nova") Expedition, 1910*, London, British
87: 22   Museum (Natural History), vol. 1 (1915), no. 3, p. 85–124. The
          Queensland Witness is fictitious.

90: 15–17 Christopher Ash, *Whaler's Eye* (New York, Macmillan, 1962), p. 68.

95: 1–2   Owen Chase, *Narrative of the Most Extraordinary and Distressing
          Shipwreck of the Whale-Ship Essex, of Nantucket; Which Was At-
          tacked and Finally Destroyed by a Large Spermaceti-Whale, in the
          Pacific Ocean; with an Account of the Unparalleled Sufferings of the
          Captain and Crew during a Space of Ninety-three Days at Sea, in
          Open Boats in the Years 1819 & 1820* (New York: W. B. Gillfy, 1821;
          reprinted 1963 by Corinth Books, New York), p. 25 in reprint.

95: 15–19 Clement Cleveland Sawtell, *The Ship* Ann Alexander *of New Bedford,
          1805–1851* (Mystic, Conn.: Marine Historical Association, 1962),
          p. 83.

100: 9–12 Melville, *Moby-Dick*, pp. 344–345.

102: 19–25 Thomas Beale, *The Natural History of the Sperm Whale*, p. 54; the
          book is described in the Annotated Bibliography (page 206).

105: 9–15 Beale, *op. cit.*, p. 36.

106: 11   V. G. Bogorov, "Productivity of the World Ocean," *Priroda* (Lenin-
          grad), 1967, no. 10, pp. 40–46.

106: 23   Wilbert McLeod Chapman, "Food Production from the Sea and the
          Nutritional Requirements of the World." Lecture at Conference on
          Law, Organization, and Security in the Use of the Ocean, Mershon
          Social Science Program, Ohio State University, March 17–18, 1967,
          mimeographed, pp. 1–11.

107: 1   John D. Strickland, "Phytoplankton and Marine Primary Production,"
          Annual Review of Microbiology, vol. 19 (1965), pp. 127–162.

107: 4–7 Wolf Vishniac, professor of biology at the University of Rochester,
          New York, kindly sent me a copy of a letter he had written on July 14,
          1966, to the U. S. Fish and Wildlife Service, outlining his views on
          ocean productivity. In the letter he quoted Lamont C. Cole, professor
          of zoology at Cornell University, Ithaca, New York.

109: 3–13 James Thurber, "Here Come the Dolphins," *Lanterns and Lances*
          (New York: Harper and Row, 1961), pp. 151–152.

117: 19   *Star Third* and her passengers are fictitious.

REFERENCE NOTES

PAGE & LINE

120: 19–22 Loren Eiseley, "The Long Loneliness," *American Scholar*, Winter 1960–61, p. 57.

121: 26 Charles Haskins Townsend, "The Distribution of Certain Whales as through Shown by Logbook Records of American Whaleships," *Zoologica*, vol. 122: 13 19 (1935), pp. 1–50.

122: 14 *Halcón* and her crew are fictitious.

129: 9 The use of whale meat to feed screwworm maggots is described in through A. U. Spear, "Whale Attacks Fly," *Sea Frontiers*, vol. 5 (1959), 130: 5 pp. 200–204.

134: 1 The "conference" session on conservation of whales is based mainly through on:
136: 2 Noel Simon, "Of Whales and Whaling," *Science*, vol. 149 (1965), p. 943.

M. N. Tarasevich, "Distribution of Sperm Whales in the Northern Region of Kurile Waters" (in Russian), *Nauka* (Moscow), 1965, p. 42.

John Walsh, "Whales: Decline Continues Despite Limitations on Catch," *Science*, vol. 157 (1967), pp. 1024, 1025.

E. J. Slijper, "A Hundred Years of Modern Whaling," *Nederlandsche Commissie voor Internationale Natuurbescherming* (Amsterdam), Med. 19 (1965), pp. 5, 34.

Mack Laing, "Have Whalers Become too Efficient?" *Freedom from Hunger Campaign News*, FAO, United Nations (Rome), vol. 5 (1964), no. 31, p. 14.

136: 19 A photograph of this stranded whale was reproduced as plate 10 in H. through Boschma, "On the Teeth and Some Other Particulars of the Sperm 137: 2 Whale . . . ," *Temminckia* (Leyden), vol. 3 (1938).

138: 22–24 Peter Crowcroft, *Mice All Over* (London: G. T. Foulis, 1966), p. 2.

140: 21 *Shoku Maru* and her crew are fictitious.

144: 12–16 *Moby-Dick*, p. 457.

144: 18 The brief history of whaling is based on many sources, the more importhrough tant of which are:
149: 10 E. J. Slijper, *Whales* (London: Hutchinson, 1962).

F. C. Fraser, "Whales and Whaling," Sir Raymond Priestley, Raymond J. Adie, and G. de Q. Robin (eds.), *Antarctic Research: A Review of British Scientific Achievement* . . . (London: Butterworths, 1964), pp. 191–205.

N. A. Mackintosh, *The Stocks of Whales* (London: Fishing News [Books] Ltd., 1965).

PAGE & LINE

John Gulland, "The Management of Antarctic Whaling Resources," *Journal du Conseil* (Copenhagen), vol. 31 (1968), pp. 330–341.

151: 22   *Clipper Dawn* is a fictitious name.

156: 2   *Sonan Maru* and *Seki Maru* and their crews, as well as the American
through   observer, are fictitious. Japan has a real Whales Research Institute
166: 4   supported by government and industry. Whaling is described in *Japanese Whaling Industry* (Tokyo: Japan Whaling Association, 1954).

166: 5   Yoro Arai and Shigeru Sakai. "Whale Meat in Nutrition," *Scientific
through   Reports of the Whales Research Institute* (Tokyo), no. 7 (1952), p. 64.
167: 2

167: 7–10   H. R. Lillie, "With Whales and Seals," *British Medical Journal* (London), 1949, vol. ii, December 24, p. 1467.

167: 24   Albert Schweitzer, *Out of My Life and Thought: An Autobiography*
through   (New York: Holt, Rinehart, and Winston, 1949), p. 234.
168: 7

172: 13   *Sea Otter* and Sea Otter Hansen are fictitious names. Amchitka Island
through   is a real part of the National Wildlife Refuge System.
174: 14

183: 12–20 E. L. Nagel, P. J. Morgane, and W. L. McFarland, "Anesthesia for the Bottlenose Dolphin . . . ," *Science*, vol. 146 (1964), pp. 1591–1593.

183: 21–32 Vagn Flyger, "Succinylcholine Chloride for Killing or Capturing Whales," *Norwegian Whaling Gazette* (Oslo), 1964, no. 4, pp. 88–90.

184: 19   McGill and the other characters and events are fictitious.
through
186: 27

189: 19   John Cantwell and Peter Skansen are fictitious.

194: 11   Charles Haskins Townsend, "The Porpoise in Captivity," *Zoologica*, vol. 1 (1914), pp. 289–299.

Seven Whaling Classics:
A Selected and Annotated Bibliography

A dip into the wellsprings of knowledge of the cachalot or sperm whale: seven publications that appeared between 1798 and 1898.

COLNETT, JAMES. *A Voyage to the South Atlantic and round the Horn into the Pacific Ocean, for the Purpose of Extending the Spermaceti Whale Fisheries, and Other Objects of Commerce by Ascertaining the Ports, Bays, Harbours and Anchoring Berths, in certain Islands and Coasts in those Seas at which the Ships of British Merchants might be Refitted;* Undertaken and Performed by Captain James Colnett, of the Royal Navy, in the Ship *Rattler*. London: W. Bennett, 1798.

Colnett sailed from England on January 4, 1793, and returned on November 1, 1794, after twenty-two months. He did not touch at any known ports except Rio de Janeiro in going out and Saint Helena on the way home. He set forth in a little sloop of 374 tons fitted for sperm-whaling on a modest scale. Down the long east coast of South America to the Horn he went, then up the west coast to Twenty-Four North, off Baja California, then back again to England. I admire his report as a navigator's, not particularly as a naturalist's. His illustration of a young sperm whale taken off Mexico is as fanciful as an early Christian sketch of a cherubim. "Its heart," wrote Colnett, "was cooked in a sea-pye, and offered an excellent meal" (page 80).

REYNOLDS, JEREMIAH N. "Mocha Dick, or the White Whale of the Pacific." *Knickerbocker* magazine, 13 (1839), 5, 377–398. Reissued in book form with introduction and illustrations by Lowell Le Roy Balcom. New York: Charles Scribner's Sons, 1932 (page references are to this edition).

The immortal *Moby-Dick* was based in part on this story of only seventeen pages by Reynolds, a naval officer. He told of an albino sperm-whale bull that eluded capture for many years off Peru. "Opinions differ," he wrote, "as to the time of his discovery. It is settled, however, that previous to the year 1810, he had been seen and attacked near the island of Mocha. Numerous boats are known to have been shattered by his immense flukes, or ground to pieces in the crush of his powerful jaws; and, on one occasion, it is said that he came off victorious from a conflict with the crews of three English whalers, striking fiercely at the last of the retreating boats, at the moment it was rising from the water, in its hoist up to the ship's davits" (page 21).

The crew of the *Penquin* finally did Mocha Dick in. "The dying animal was struggling in a whirlpool of bloody foam, and the ocean far around was tinted crimson. 'Stern all!' I shouted, as he commenced running impetuously in a circle, beating the water alternately with his head and flukes, and smiting his teeth ferociously into their sockets, with a crashing sound, in the strong spasms of dissolution. 'Stern all! or we shall be stove!' As I gave the command, a stream of black, clotted gore rose in a thick spout above the expiring brute, and fell in a shower around, bedewing, or rather drenching us, with a spray of blood. '*There's the flag!*' I exclaimed; 'there! thick as tar! Stern! every soul of ye! He's going in his flurry!' And the monster, under the convulsive influence of his final paroxysm, flung his huge tail into the air, and then, for the space of a minute, thrashed the waters on either side of him with quick and powerful blows; the sound of the concussions resembling that of the rapid discharge of artillery. He then turned slowly and heavily on his side, and lay a dead mass upon the sea. . . ." (pages 74, 77).

BEALE, THOMAS. *The Natural History of the Sperm Whale, to Which Is Added a Sketch of a South-Sea Whaling Voyage.* London: John van Voorst, 1839.

Thomas Beale, "Surgeon, Demonstrator of Anatomy to the Eclectic Society of London, etc., and Late Surgeon to the *Kent* and *Sarah and Elizabeth*, South Seamen," dedicated his book to a friend who had struggled "to liberate the Negro from the condition of the slave—efforts which were commenced many years since, and at a time too, when to attempt to break his chains was considered the index of a weak or flighty intellect" (page vi).

Beale sailed in the whaler *Kent* down the Atlantic coast of South America to the Horn, then up the Pacific to the Sandwich (Hawaiian) Islands, then west to the Spice Islands, Kamchatka, and other landfalls of the North Pacific. At midnight in 1892 he secretly left the ship in the Bonin Islands, appalled by the tyranny of her captain, and boarded the whaler *Sarah and Elizabeth*, in which he sailed down to the Horn again and back to England after fifty thousand miles under sail.

Ever a keen observer, Beale gave a luminous account of the anatomy and behavior of the sperm whale. Though scientists now have better information, they still turn gratefully to his diary of observations of whale behavior—the intimate glimpses that men in modern, noisy motor ships can rarely obtain.

BENNETT, FREDERICK DEBELL. *Narrative of a Whaling Voyage around the Globe from the Year 1833 to 1836.* London: Richard Bentley, 1840. 2 vols.

Bennett, a Fellow of the Royal College of Surgeons, went to sea on the *Tuscan* in 1833 "to investigate the anatomy and habits of Southern Whales, and the mode of

BIBLIOGRAPHY

conducting the Sperm Whale Fishery, a subject then untouched by the literature of any country" (volume 1, page v). His report sparkles with the excitement of a naturalist turned loose in a new world. Besides a priceless account of the primitive peoples of Polynesia, the Indian Archipelago, and Baja California, he left sixty-five printed pages on the natural history of the sperm whale. The hardy men of the *Tuscan* captured seventy-eight of these beasts during their three-year cruise.

Melville wrote: "There are only two books in being which at all pretend to put the living Sperm Whale before you, and at the same time in the remotest degree succeed in the attempt. Those books are Beale's and Bennett's, both in their time surgeons to English South-Sea whale-ships, and both exact and reliable men" (*Moby-Dick*, page 130).

MELVILLE, HERMAN. *The Whale.* London: Richard Bentley, 1851. *Moby-Dick.* New York: Harper and Brothers, 1851.

The Whale was first published in an edition of five hundred copies in England in October 1851, and republished in America later the same year as *Moby-Dick.* Melville himself described it as "a romance of adventure founded upon certain wild legends in the Southern Sperm Whale Fisheries, and illustrated with the author's own personal experiences, of two years or more, as a harpooner" (*Moby-Dick*, page x). The book was far ahead of its time. In the first thirty-five years after its publication, fewer than two thousand copies were sold. Now it is seen as a great American novel and is always in print.

The story of the hero-monster white as snow was based in part on Melville's observations at sea, and in part on Reynolds' "Mocha Dick," but it also drew heavily on Shakespeare and the Bible. "Whatever Melville read he piratically made his own, extending, deepening, and embellishing his thefts so that no literary judge can but approve and applaud," wrote editors Luther S. Mansfield and Howard P. Vincent in the richly annotated centennial edition of *Moby-Dick* (page 571), published by Hendricks House, New York, in 1952. (Page references to *Moby-Dick* in the present book refer to this edition.)

SCAMMON, CHARLES MELVILLE. *The Marine Mammals of the Northwestern Coast of North America*, Described and Illustrated together with an Account of the American Whale-Fishery. San Francisco: John H. Carmany, 1874. Reprinted, with an introduction, largely biographical, by Victor B. Scheffer. New York: Dover, 1968.

Scammon followed the gold-seekers to California in 1850, then turned to his first love, the sea. His early efforts as a natural history writer were published in the *Overland Monthly*, 1869–1872, along with sketches by Mark Twain and Bret Harte. His curiosity about the sea led him at last to write a book in which he tried "to give as correct figures of the different species of marine mammals . . . as could be obtained from a careful study of them from life, and numerous measurements after death. . . ." (page 11). The unsold copies of Scammon's beautiful work were lost in the San Francisco earthquake and fire of 1906. His name lives on in the Scammon Lagoon of modern maps, a place where a century ago he spied out the secret mating waters of the gray whale.

BULLEN, FRANK T. *The Cruise of the Cachalot; Round the World after Sperm Whales.* London: Smith, Elder and Co., 1898.

Bullen was an English immigrant to America, a "lime-juicer." At the age of eighteen, and surely not aware of what he was doing, he signed on as a seaman aboard the filthy whaler *Cachalot* out of New Bedford. She circumnavigated the globe, and before the end of the cruise, Bullen became first mate.

According to the zoologist Ralph S. Palmer, the voyage was begun in 1875 but the account was written many years later.* This seems likely, for the style of the writing is mature. Though I bought my valued copy of Bullen's book in the juvenile section of a book shop, I agree with the author that it is "in no sense exclusively a book for boys."

* Ralph S. Palmer, "A School of Whales, Kogia?" *Journal of Mammalogy,* vol. 29 (1948), no. 4, p. 421.

Index

INDEX

INDEX

About the Author

Victor B. Scheffer specialized in the study of marine mammals as a biologist with the United States Fish and Wildlife Service in Seattle, Washington, from 1937 to 1969. He has lectured at the University of Washington on wildlife ecology and on the natural history of vertebrates. He received his Ph.D. from the University of Washington in 1936, is a member of Sigma Xi and Phi Beta Kappa, and received the United States Department of Interior's Distinguished Service Award in 1965. Dr. Scheffer was awarded the John Burroughs Medal (1970) for the year's best book in natural history, *The Year of the Whale*. His most recent book is *The Year of the Seal*.

About the Illustrator

Leonard Everett Fisher has illustrated over 100 books, including a number in the field of science; some of these he has written himself. A native New Yorker, he studied at the Heckscher Foundation, the Art Students League, and the studio of Moses and Raphael Soyer. He was awarded the Pulitzer Art Prize in 1950. In addition to the decorations for *The Year of the Whale*, Mr. Fisher provided the drawings for *The Year of the Seal*.